LUCKY ICONS

To John Seaton,
in appreciation!
of a wonderful trip
to New Sabounen, Ohio
and back

Blessings
BEVERLEY Rose Enright
August 1, 2017

LUCKY ICONS

Beverley Rose Enright

Library of Congress Control Number: 2012918679
ISBN: Hardcover   978-1-4797-2875-6
                 Softcover   978-1-4797-2874-9
                 Ebook   978-1-4797-2876-3

This book was printed in the United States of America.

To order additional copies of this book, contact:
Xlibris Corporation
1-888-795-4274
www.Xlibris.com
Orders@Xlibris.com
118710

Contents

Icon Poems

Extinct Birds

Family Memorials

Calculus Sonnets

Sonnets To The Psalms

Poems On The Twenty-Third Psalm

Nature And Environment

Strawberry Variations

Bovine Beauties

Parodies

Art, People, & Math

Songs

Misshelved

I'm a book of verse
that's been misshelved
so no one can ever find me.
Readers of poetry see my title
and number in the catalogue,
but when they look in that place
I'm not there!
O God, it's not fair!
How did it happen?
Perhaps it comes of never
knowing my place,
always wandering, moving
from flower to flower
like a butterfly.
Or maybe I'm just
predestined to be lost,
closed in an eternal cocoon,
hidden under the dust
of actuarial tables,
revenues, and costs,
or stuck in between
the signs and numbers
of astrological careers.
I try to cry out
as the eyes go by,
O see, see poetical me!
Pull me out, open me,
and read with delight.
Put me down on a table
right out in sight!
I am so full of music,

laughter, and tears.
Parrots squawk from my pages,
rabbits hop, thunder rages,
breezes blow a soft snow,
leaves rustle old tunes—
come giggle and dance
and give me
one more chance.

ICON POEMS

Icons, Icons

The icons on my computer screen
take me to any tool or place
for a fulfillment of any dream
or any desire in cyberspace.

I click on the icon for the word processor
and here I am with an empty page.
I can choose a font only a typesetter
would have when I was a younger age.

The miracles of technology
brought forth from minds of men
enable me to type poetry
and print up a book or thousands.

How do we use computer tools
for the betterment of humankind?
How to make sure who makes the rules
has everyone's life in mind?

At the Corcoran Gallery in DC
I once was in a roomful of icons
from Russia, and my son, then three,
cried out to me excitedly,
"Oh, Mommy, look! Lucky icons!"

"A window into heaven" for us to see
the glory of God when we look upon
these pictures painted so lovingly
which bless everyone with lucky icons.

Saint John The Forerunner

"Prepare the way of the Lord", he called
after forty days in the wilderness,
and those who heard his voice were awed
by the power of John the Baptist.

After forty days in the wilderness,
clothed in a shirt of camel hair,
appeared with power, John the Baptist,
spiritually filled with faith and prayer.

Clothed in a shirt of camel hair,
and lean from eating insects and honey,
but spiritually filled with faith and prayer,
came forth this figure unlike any.

Lean from eating insects and honey,
"The Messiah is coming!" he cried aloud.
This came from a figure unlike any.
Some ran to spread his fame abroad.

"The Messiah is coming!" he cried aloud,
and people fell down on their knees.
Some ran to spread his fame abroad,
while he baptized others until he sees

the people rise up from their knees.
Jesus was walking toward the shore,
where John baptized until he sees
as he lifted the water up to pour

that Jesus was walking toward the shore
requesting that He should be baptized.
But as the Baptist began to pour,
a dove descended from the skies.

Jesus requested He be baptized,
and a voice from heaven for all to hear,
as the dove descended from the skies,
made the people know that God was near.

A voice from heaven for all to hear
said, "This is my beloved Son,"
and the people knew that God was near.
"Behold the Lamb of God," said John.

"Jesus is my beloved Son"
Christ had come there to redeem.
"Behold the Lamb of God," said John.
Salome danced for her mother's scheme.

Christ had come there to redeem,
but John would suffer a martyr's fate
when Salome danced for her mother's scheme
to get John's head upon a plate.

John would suffer a martyr's fate
for like Christ he called men from their sins.
John's severed head was on a plate,
but the icons show who really wins.

Christ saved believers from their sins,
and those who heard His voice were awed.
The icons show who really wins.
"Prepare the way of the Lord!" John called.

Archangel With The Golden Hair

This angel haloed with gold hair
in braided curls around her face
shines with peace and loving care.
This angel haloed with gold hair
has large dark eyes that softly stare
straight deep into your wounded place,
this angel haloed with gold hair
in braided curls around her face.

Old Testament Trinity

If I peel away with knowledge, skill, and care,
each of the blackened varnished layers of centuries
of repaintings on the icon of my faith, Rublev,
O beloved Andrei Rublev, will I at last find you?
Or have the *Kommissars* taken over my hands
and axed them into pieces and burned them in the fires
of their blasphemy? Wherever you are, painting still
in glory, in the communion of saints, reach down
your arms to me and make my hands your hands again.

Three men seated at a round table, and I
at a table nearby, trying to do homework as I recite
the twenty-third psalm, falling deep in Plato's cave
of shadows, and I overhear the mocking, "fighting" words,
to become a creature of the shadows, a cornered animal
that trapped strikes! O why did I remain?
Why did I not leave immediately when they came?
Three men came in, sat down together, and I saw
the shadow world of the meanness, the crumminess,
and heard the mock of Satan, and I laughed his laugh,
even as I recited the twenty-third psalm. Three angels
seated round a table in your window into heaven, Rublev,
and I can see it now. But not then . . . not then.

O icon master, I am now but your broken egg yolk.
Use me, use me to paint again the Holy Mother of sorrows
on this Mother's Day of 1984, her sacred heart ringed
with roses, and the blessed child at her cheek.
I am only your poor broken golden egg yolk, beloved hand,
into which you pour your holy water, mix your pigments,
your finely powdered colors, then dip your brush
to paint the icon of this great Christian faith forever.

Blessed Andrei Rublev's Trinity

Three angels came to Abraham.
They sit in a circle, three in one.
He fetched them milk and a bit of lamb.
Three angels came to Abraham,
and Sarah laughed, "How old I am!"
when they told him Sarah would bear a son.
Three angels came to Abraham.
They sit in a circle, three in one.

The Holy Face

A miraculous imprint of Christ
was etched on a square of white linen
that was pressed when held to His face.
This legend is not in the Gospels
and is told in a few different ways.
One is that Christ appeared to a prince
sick unto death, who entreated of Jesus
to heal his body and then asked for a sign,
a proof of Christ's presence on cloth.
Another tells of a woman on the way
Jesus walked and carried the cross up the mount.
She pressed her cloth to His face
to wipe off the blood and the sweat,
but the print showed no blood or the marks
of the brutal scourging or thorns
that circled his brow, all erased,
as if it revealed the foretold risen face.
Other names for this icon exist:
"Veronica," "Mandylion," "The Face of Christ
Not Created by Human Hand."
But an artist's hand painted the icon,
often on linen that was glued to the wood.
The artist had fasted and prayed
that the Spirit of God would take over his hand
as he painted Christ's Holy Face.

Saint George The Dragonslayer

An icon purely allegorical
because Saint George the martyr after all
never met a dragon actually
while seated on a white horse naturally
is still an image of the spirit's fight
and triumph over evil force despite
the world's tyrannies and unseen power
that fills hearts of people with fear and terror.
George fought for Christ with his great strength,
and was beheaded for his Christian faith
by Diocletian, but a legend grew
into the icon that tells with a view
how he saved a wailing kingdom from
a dragon's fiery threat to overcome
and take a princess for a sacrifice
with one thrust of his spear from paradise.
So the souls that struggle with the terror
of persecution and temptation's error
to yield to Satan and the doom of hell
can be saved and with saints in heaven dwell.

Mother Of God
Of The Burning Bush

Fall leaves flame reddest on the burning bush,
a shrub named like the icon's holy view
of past Red persecution's crush
against the Church. New changes can't undo
all the destruction of the churches, nor hush
the anger and regret, the grief that grew
from chopped and burning icons, that fatal rush
of fanatic revolutionaries against the glue
of old communities. Those forest fires
burned out and now the roots send up new trees.
New icons and new churches now aspire,
reclaim the fearful spirit hiding, seize
the keys to the kingdom's glorious light
where love and mercy triumph over might.

Saint Christopher The Dog Headed, And Sheila, The Dog Who Loved Me

Icons exist of a curious saint
With a body of a man dressed for a fight,
But with the head of a dog
In a halo of light.

It's bogus, a mistake, write the scholars.
The painters used literally a description
Of what was an ignorant metaphor
For an area strange and unknown.

Saint Christopher came from a region
At the edge of what was the known world.
At the edge people said were odd folk,
"Cannibals, Cyclops, and dog headed".

How could those monks get it so wrong?
After all the prayers and fasting?
After the blessing of their paints and their brushes?
After the Divine Spirit moved their hands?

And here opens the crack to dangerous doubt
To darken all icons, stain with disbelief
Those heavenly windows, view as vain illusions
From lives in a web of deceit.

Yet those who love dogs would protest
That dogs too can be saints and their acts
Save lives, heal hearts, make miracles come true,
Even at supreme sacrifice.

I read a recent newspaper account
Of a Chihuahua who held off a pit bull
At the cost of his life to protect
A four-year-old boy till help came.

There are dogs who can smell early cancer,
Dogs who warn of coming catastrophes.
Dogs who can find their way home across continents.
Dogs lead the blind and catch thieves.

I never warmed to dogs; they were loud,
Jumping all over, their nose in your butt,
(You had to be careful not to step in their poop)
Sloppy kisses, and smelly dog-breath.

In spite of all that, my daughter's dog, Sheila,
Decided to love me and show me how dogs
Can conquer your heart with true love
That lasts long after they are put down.

Surely there's a heaven somewhere for Sheila
Where angels now throw her the ball
She can catch in mid-air as she jumps for it always
To bring it back to be thrown up again.

Surely there's a heaven somewhere for Sheila
Like the one my heart sees through these tears
Like her tears of joy when she jumped at my coming
After a long time away on a trip.

How she stood on her hind legs to dance
With her paws on my shoulders like a human
As if in comfort to me for my loss
When my husband left me for another.

Saint Montfort was a dog who was killed
With blood on his mouth and the cradle,
Before they found the baby unhurt,
And the dead rat, wolf, or snake nearby.

Pilgrims came to his grave as to a shrine,
And tales were told of the healings
As if he had been, well, divine,
Possessing a soul that was human.

Saint Christopher wasn't dog-headed,
And the Catholics had him decanonized
Now he's a myth, and his statues and medals
No more adorn necks and top dashboards.

And what of his dog headed icons?
I view them affectionately.
They're a window into heaven where Sheila
Again brings her wet ball back to me.

The Archangel Gabriel

Robed in gold with a cape of green
the Archangel Gabriel is always seen
standing on the right on the gates to God
reflecting Archangel Michael standing on the left.
Archangel Gabriel stands on the left
facing Virgin Mary seated on the right
in the Annunciation of the coming birth
of God's Holy Son to live on earth.

The Archangel Michael

You ride in fire for your wings are aflame
on a red-winged horse with a fiery mane.
Candle flames dance on the tips of your wings,
and crimson flickers on the lips of your wings,
for I know you now as I knew you then
by the red, bloodred of your light.
You've come for the goats and that goat-footed man
with the hook in his throat
and his eyes all pewter rimmed with rust
who would drag me down to the dust.
A volcanic fire in the blue-black night,
you hold the Bible with your lance of truth;
you blow the horn of the Day of Judgment;
you summon all the souls of the earth.

Icon Of Christ In Glory

This vision was told by Ezekiel,
and again by Saint John the Divine.
Four creatures with wings fill the corners;
holding their scriptures, they shine.

This vision shows rainbows encircling,
translucently colored like jewels,
on clouds soft as lambs wool in springtime
which billow like ripples in pools.

This vision has choirs of angels,
and elders with lamp stands aflame,
and six-winged seraphim, singing,
all praising the Almighty's Name.

This vision of gold radiating
around the white garments of light
shows God, Spirit, Christ, One in union
enthroned in majestical might.

EXTINCT BIRDS

In The Land Of The Extinct Birds

a series of poems in forms

Prelude

I fly in my wing chair
    fueled only with words
from a book to the land
    of the extinct birds.

I've my paint box and brushes,
    my dreams and my wishes,
my colored pencils and papers
    from the land of skyscrapers.

I've come to the shore
    of that historical place
to see and explore
    what we cannot replace.

[NOTE: The book referred to in the first stanza is
Vanished Species by David Day, London editions, 1981.]

A Dirge For The Dodo

Three centuries, three centuries,
    And it will be centuries more,
The Dodo means extinction,
    Lost relic of aging lore.

Fat and round and fifty pounds,
    And it will be centuries more,
The Dodo had a massive beak,
    Lost relic of aging lore.

Naked head half veiled with fuzz,
    And it will be centuries more,
The Dodo had small flightless wings,
    Lost relic of aging lore.

Diamond eyes and downy feathers,
    And it will be centuries more,
The Dodo had a three-plumed tail,
    Lost relic of aging lore.

Laid single eggs and swallowed stones,
    And it will be centuries more,
The largest pigeon that ever lived,
    Lost relic of aging lore.

Three centuries, three centuries,
    And it will be centuries more,
The Dodo means extinction,
    Lost relic of aging lore.

Elegy To The Elephant Bird

The largest bird that ever lived on earth
Endured millenniums over thirty times
The duration of human existence's length,
Protected by its size and tropic climes.

At ten feet tall, it weighed over half a ton.
Its massive legs and taloned claws and beak
Shaped like a sword caused fear to look upon.
No predator but one though small and weak

Could threaten its dominion and it reigned,
The Lords of Madagascar, until men
Entered its island forest home and aimed
Their capture at the eggs extinguishing them.

And oh! What eggs they were to startle sight!
The French and Dutch and Portuguese seamen
Of the sixteenth century eagerly sought
These curios to sell to merchantmen.

The circumference of these eggs could swallow up
Three times the eggs of the largest dinosaurs.
The yolk swam in nine liters; its omelet
Was more than sixteen dozen eggs of ours.

The birds retreated to the forest core
As burning, cutting, clearing musket bearers
Drove them into hiding from the shore,
Took eggs and habitat, the fatal errors.

Merchants and pirates care not to record,
To observe or preserve exotic birds,
And when their remotest last abode was gored,
Too late Gutenberg sent out the words.

The Island of Madagascar is a tomb
For many extinct species, and its girth
Is witness to when men could not make room
For the largest birds that ever lived on earth.

Memorium To The Moa

The moas are all gone away.
Maori did not kill them all
tripping with slings of cords and balls
around their legs in deadly play.

The tallest birds that ever lived
hid in islands of New Zealand,
away from the exposing sand.
in thickest woods they yet conceived,

laying eggs to feed a tribe
of natives that buried a chief with one
sitting in his lap so lone
exhumed intact with chick inside.

They lasted fifty years beyond
the eighteenth century so that
an English scientist in fact
could study, write, and even send

reports and drawings, measurements
to awe the ornithologists.
The Royal Academy exists
to spread the news of such immense,

rare, and wingless birds to men
who care to read about such strange
creatures still alive to change
their worldview of kind and kin.

But settlers sinned and were too quick
for flocks of birds too thinned and shy
to procreate and that is why
the naturalists could not protect.

And what is left for me to say?
Not even in the Royal Zoo
could some be shipped for public view.
The moas are all gone away.

Pantoum For The Pigeon Hollandaise

The Pigeon Hollandaise was colored deep blue,
a deep marine blue, with a hot pepper tail,
and a scarlet ellipse around its eye too,
with white crest and breast like a hood of chain mail.

A deep marine blue with a hot pepper tail,
as delicious to eat as it was to behold,
with its white crest and breast like a hood of chain mail,
its white beak was tipped with a coin of gold.

As delicious to eat as it was to behold,
its feet were red, but a butter-sauced yellow
tipped its white beak with a coin of gold.
Oh, this graceful bird was a tropical fellow!

Its feet were red, but a butter-sauced yellow
attracted the hunters, cats, dogs, other pests.
Oh, this graceful bird was a tropical fellow,
but it was the pet monkeys that raided the nests.

It wasn't the hunters, cats, dogs, other pests
that came to live on Mauritius Island,
but it was the pet monkeys that raided the nests,
that killed off the very last specimen.

When men came to live on Mauritius Island,
and then ceased to see the red-circled eye, too,
they were blind to the death of the very last specimen
of the Pigeon Hollandaise, colored deep blue.

Rondeau For The Rodriguez Solitaire

A bird of beauty rare with swollen breasts
where feathers whiter were and bosoms dressed.
Their dances graced displays with wing tips knobbed
that rattled, clapped, and whirred the short wings bobbed.
Their long and slender necks rose from their chest.

Mating for life like other doves that nest
with but one chick, they fed and cared obsessed
and drove away all others. When caught, they sobbed,
a bird of beauty rare.

Their slender beaks, a widow's peak, moustache
of darker brown adorned their face and pressed
above their nostrils prettily and daubed
a darker line around their eyes. We're robbed
because they were as lovely to the taste,
a bird of beauty rare.

Pushkin Sonnet For The Laysan Millerbird

Laysan is an outer island in Hawaii.
The Millerbird that lived there was a warbler,
blest with a song as liquid as the sea,
as full of melody as a happy bugler.

Its favorite food was moths that were named "millers",
and especially they liked the caterpillars.
They were so tame they'd land on a person's head,
and flocks showed up at meals to be fed.

But that was early on in 1913,
the year the rabbits were brought to the island
which soon became a barren waste of sand.

Such a desert that the lake's bright sheen
seemed a mirage for all the life was gone,
despondent whispers replaced the lost song.

Blues For Brace's Emerald Hummingbird

You know a hummingbird is a bird that hums.
Yep, a hummingbird's a bird that hums,
an electric guitar as big as your thumb.

But a hummingbird's not a bird that sings.
I say a hummingbird's not a bird that sings.
That sound he makes is his whirring wings.

Well, a hummingbird is a bird so small,
Yep, a hummingbird is a bird so small,
It sips the nectar through a syringelike straw.

Man, this hummingbird is colored bright.
I say this hummingbird is neon bright,
a living jewel shot through with light.

Well, this emerald bird's without a sound.
You know this emerald bird's no longer around.
The stuffed one's the same as the fossils found.

Oh, it's niche was so small in the 1800's,
I say it's numbers so little as the 1800's
closed, it dropped to zero numbers.

Well, Lewis Brace found just this one bird.
I say Lewis Brace found this now stuffed bird.
That's why we know, and how we heard.

But I wonder if we could have saved those lives,
and turned a relict bird into one that thrives.

A Limerick For The Laughing Owl

There once were large owls in New Zealand,
Whekaus of the North and South Islands.
    They chuckled; they cooed;
    They whistled; they mewed;
Hysterically laughed as they left with their woodlands.

Rubaiyat For India's Pink-Headed Duck

North of the Ganges and west Brahmaputra,
Wings whistling softly, the drake's mellow "waugh-uh"
Amid the loud quacking in the ponds and the lakes,
Grasslands, the floodplains, with crocs, and with tigras,

Humans hunted these ducks all year so it takes
Just forty years to drop abundant drakes
To ten, which can't breed in an English park
Far from their swamps and their native brake.

A rosy pink head was its distinctive mark,
And it laid global eggs, white balls in the dark,
With shell pink underwings and its bill lovely pink,
Its long neck like the crescent moon's vanishing arc.

Haiku For The Ryukyu Kingfisher

Wings of peacock jade
send a flaming scarlet spear
deep into the sea.

Seguidilla For The Saint Kitts Puerto Rican Bullfinch

The "Mountain Blacksmith" sings
   Like cardinals trill
In seven notes that spring
   From a big bill
Where tiny hammers ring
   A silver anvil.
   The monkeys wrest
The red head and black wings
   And rob the nest.

A Glosa For
The Lord Howe Island White Eye

Innocence is green and gold
so she was told.

—from *"Innocence Is Green and Gold"*
by Beverley Rose Hoskins

Great numbers perched in Kentia palms
and on the wooded hills they told
their powerful songs in day-long psalms,
Innocence is green and gold,

Mostly green with golden-yellowed
throat and white ringed eyes and fold
of feathers lining nests rats swallowed
long ago, *so she was told.*

Sestina For
The Stephen Island Wren

Not far from New Zealand's South Island
lies a small wooded island named Stephen.
It once was the home of wee wrens
that were cute little birds with fanned wings
as big as their bodies, and tails mothlike
cut short to roll in your palm, but a cat—

Yes, it was but one solitary cat
that came to this secluded island
with a lighthouse keeper, and like
he'd brought snakes to slither over Stephen,
this cat caught all those birds with weak wings
as they scurried at night. These rare wrens

ran more like young mice than like wrens,
and they lived in rock holes, so the cat
could easy catch those who took wing
while he freely explored the whole island.
Like a cougar chasing chicks, he roamed Stephen.
The keeper and collectors all alike

watched and reported on these birds so unlike
other species of birds and small wrens
from the lands across oceans from Stephen,
where birds can fly fast from a cat.
Such predators were unknown to this island.
Birds had simply no need for strong wings.

On South Island lived birds with no wings
peculiar to only New Zealand, much like
the moas, all killed when men came to the island.
It was less than a year for the wrens
to become all extinct by this cat
that was brought to the lighthouse on Stephen.

As the mob that threw stones at Saint Stephen,
blindly watched as his spirit took wing,
Saul crouched with his eyes like a cat
but was scared on the road so much like
the timid and meek little wrens
that disappeared in one year from that island.

Why did those men who came to Stephen Island
like that cat so much to let it stay
and slay all the wrens as they could not wing away?

Heroic Couplets For
The Heath Hen

They bred and fed in groups one thousand strong
or more; in Spring the male birds in mating's song
"boomed" out noisily their dance and strut,
displaying to female birds their fan-ringed butts
with flaring feathers and swelled bright orange necks,
a giant mass of troops entreating sex.
When early settlers to New England found
them everywhere upon the brushy ground
of Boston, they were shot so constantly
that servants were told by cooks to see
that Heath Hen was not on the table everyday,
but only a few times a week. To slay
so many birds so fast, the numbers fell
quite quickly. The Long Islanders proposed a bill
for a closed season to preserve Heath Hen.
But when the Act was read, the members said
they could not see the reason, as they misread,
"For preserving Indians or other heathen."
The overhunting did only partly threaten
the Heath Hen's dwindling numbers; their ground nests
made them vulnerable to many pests,
dogs, cats, and rats, and new predators. Disease
from old world chickens, pheasants, seized
in epidemics native birds, and then
the final blow to end their kind came when
the prairie was converted into farmland.

By 1830 none lived on the mainland,
but still were found in Martha's Vineyard island
in Massachusetts; a small band
of birds grew smaller yet, falling to less
than fifty when a reservation, yes,
sixteen hundred acres was set up,
and numbers did a two thousand higher jump.
But then in 1916 came a fire
that burned the breeding area entire.
It was followed by a winter so severe,
that but one hundred fifty birds lived there.
And then Blackhead disease brought in by turkeys
reduced the number down to but thirteen
that further fell to two, and 1930
did see just one Heath Hen that narrowly
escaped a passing car delaying fate
just two more years, because without a mate
the Heath Hen joined the company of birds
that passed into extinction from great herds.

Villanelle For
The Painted Vulture

The painted vulture's wings and tail were white
with brown; its long soft ruff could hide its head.
The natives used wing quills to make peace-pipes.

The bare skin of the head and neck had stripes
of loosely wrinkled purple, yellow, red.
The colors sparked the wings' and tail's white.

The stomach hung, a pouch of reddish light
until it bulged from roasted reptiles fed.
The natives used wing quills to make peace pipes.

It had white legs and feet, a yellow bill fit tight
from the purple cheeks beneath the crown of red.
The painted vulture's wings and tail were white.

When fires flamed the Florida meadows bright,
flocks of these vultures searched for burning dead
snakes, lizards, leaving quills to make peace pipes.

The eighteenth century's Florida frosts did smite
severely the white tender toes, and spread
these perished vultures' wings and tails so white
the natives used wing quills to make peace pipes.

A Ballad For
The American Ivory-Billed Woodpecker

Vast timberlands throughout the South
    Can no more be found.
That's why this giant woodpecker
    No longer makes a sound.

The loss of habitat's not all
    That made it disappear.
Hunters and collectors too
    Make us shed a tear.

A striking twenty inches long
    "Van Dyke" to Audubon,
Four hundred specimens exist
    Although the bird is gone.

Indians had used its beak for trade
    And its red crest, white wings
Contrasting with the black striped back
    And tail feathered things.

Alexander Wilson wrote
    That once he wounded one
And kept it in his hotel room
    When he went for a run.

When he returned into his room
    The bird made such a shout
Of grief because the man had caught
    It trying to get out.

The bird had pecked into the wall
        Near where the ceiling starts
Exposing fifteen inches square
        Of lath and plaster parts.

A fist wide hole had been pecked through
        Into the weatherboards.
One hour more it would have reached
        What it was pecking towards.

Though wounded it would get away
        But that was not to be.
It'd been discovered and it screamed
        In all its heart and beauty.

Each pair of birds needed a spread
        Two thousand acres wide
Of mature river-bottom forest
        To live and breed and hide.

Vast timberlands throughout the South
        Can no more be found.
That's why this giant woodpecker
        No longer makes a sound.

Golden Section Thirteener For The Guadeloupe Amazon

Hen-sized parrots that had a duck-like flight,
    they lived on a small island.
Iridescent purple feathers bright,
    a red, green, yellow blend,
the "roses" on the wings, a striking sight

with red around the eyes, black beak and feet,
    they attracted merchants, slaves
and settlers clearing forests, hunting meat,
    for no bird-lover staves
the slaughter and loss of forests that complete
    the wipe-out no one saves.
No island paradise could long escape
the Tropics' spread of slave plantation's rape.

Black Cauldron Anthem For The Great Auk

Thousands of thousands and ten times thousands
Which no man could number over the islands
In the North Atlantic and especially Funk Island
Where they brought the great black cauldron.

Thousands of thousands of black-headed penguins
Were stunned and grabbed and cast
Into the boiling brine for to gather
Thousands of thousands pounds of feathers.

The naked corpses fed the fire and thousands
Of thousands were tossed on the sand
To slide into the sea with the tides.
Mercy, mercy. I sigh, but there was none.

We still have geese and ducks, and yet
Why wipe out the great auk for feather beds?
Why not let some of them live and be?
They decomposed silently, eternally, in the sea.

I ask those men (we know their names)
Who quickly killed that last breeding pair,
Who stomped the egg, oh why oh why oh
Did cruel fate lead them there? Why the heel?
Why the hate? Why passion to exterminate?

Auk, auk, auk, and when one last stuffed auk
Brought the highest price ever paid at auction
For a stuffed bird specimen, up come the questions:
What was the threat? What was the fear?
Is there regret? Is there a tear?

Twin Triolets For The Carolina Parakeet

There were so many in the woods
And in the orchards that came after
That angry farmers shot the floods.
There were so many in the woods
Of yellow green sparked with orange hoods,
They killed entire flocks in laughter.
There were so many in the woods
And in the orchards that came after.

We look at the stuffed birds and brood
On beauty lost forever after.
They fed on grain and orchard foods.
We look at the stuffed birds and brood
How nuisance numbers of winged roods
Provoked fate's fatal human grafter.
We look at the stuffed birds and brood
On beauty lost forever after.

Passing-Away Stanza For The Passenger Pigeon

Flocks of two hundred million each
once blocked the sun.
Flocks of two hundred million each
were gunned to none.

Family Memorials

Father, Kenneth Montgomery Hoskins (died at age 50)

Brother, Earl Joseph Hoskins (died at age 37)

Grandmother, Rose Daetwyler Frobish (died at age 91)

Uncle, John Robert Frobish (died at age 80)

Husband for 32 years, James Michael Enright (died at age 67)

Mother, Marie Frobish Hoskins (died at age 96)

Round Was Your Face

All that you left me, Daddy,
and all that I have of yours
is a novel manuscript,
fragmented and unfinished,
and a cigar box containing letters
from your French teacher,
who wrote you every day,
a spoon, some dried rose petals,
and a few poems.
One poem in particular reads:
"Beverley, Beverley, Beverley Rose,
nobody, nobody, nobody knows
how I love my Beverley Rose."
You once told me I was
your angel of light who came to you
in your despairing loneliness,
and told you I would make it all
come right for you, but I really couldn't.
Your fingers were stained with tobacco
and cigarette burns, and your health
destroyed with alcohol, drugs,
shock treatments that hunched your back.
Passionate and frighteningly unstable,
you once recited to me in English
and French "The Owl and The Pussycat"
with unforgettable drama
to keep your beaten heart still beating.
It stopped, and an assassin's bullet
killed the president.
He was your hope,
and Roman Catholicism,
that black bead rosary
swaddled your bled body.

Low mass was for him in the morning,
and high mass was for you in the evening,
that day the nation mourned.
"Round is the world," you wrote,
"but every man has his corner."
Yes, they tucked you in a corner
called a mental hospital.
I cried and cracked and went there
looking for you, only to see
your life was not my life,
and all my heart and mind
could not reach around
the irrational circumference
of your reason.

Blue Roses Grow On Brother's Grave

The coffin concaves down to drop
into the freshly dug concave up,
and this meager mourning family set
watches as one golden maple leaf
slowly drifts its head upon your lid.

We were schoolchildren once
and teachers' pets. I always first
and you but one year behind me,
best in the class too.
We slipped a little in junior high.
I flirted with Elvis and rock,
and you dreamed of motorbikes and cars,
but we still clung to school and the Baptist church.
In ninth grade you decided to fail and turn delinquent,
and all your life since has been
a rotting-away dance with death.
What a beautiful boy you were, Brother,
practicing the family violin,
or making up comic routines with me,
and our exaggerated laughs and grins.
The Laurel and Hardy movies and those old radio shows
could not have foretold how tragic and fatal
was your fancy for gangs and crime,
and the madness, drinking, and debauch of your decline.
Again and again we and others
tried to give you and your life a new route;
Again and again you reclaimed the old story
of what you and your life were about.
Justice concaves down like a coffin,
and mercy concaves up like a grave,
but you were a long time a-dying,
and hope hung many times on your cross.

What a sad stinkweed life to live, Brother,
blessed with all that beauty and brain.
What a hard heartbreaker you were, Brother,
as you killed us again and again.

But if death is a spiraling function
that spins through the fires of love
burning away all but the beauty
that beats in birth and rebirth,
then you will reach heaven as handsome
as the shy boy who once graced the earth.

Keeping Up
The Standards

Her name was Rose,
and the tiniest whitest thorniest rose
she was.
She was first up
every morning to squeeze
fresh orange juice or cut
grapefruit sections.
"I'd rather cook for ten hungry men,"
and she did, so we had lots of leftovers.
She was last to retire at night,
crocheting, embroidering,
or piecing quilt blocks,
sitting near her bed
beside the dining room wall,
until after we'd all gone upstairs.
She ruled us all
and henpecked Grandpa
about every flaw,
making sure
his shirts and pants were always pressed,
and the collars and cuffs always starched,
and his favorite custard pie always baked
at all celebrations and holidays.
Her bluestocking view was that if
you could not get the menfolk to do something,
you did it yourself.
So she wired the house,
and enclosed the front porch,
and Grandpa would brag on her about it,
and she would voice her displeasure at that.

She was so in the habit of making do
she even sewed patches over the holes
in the toes of my tennis shoes.
She was a recluse
and seldom went out
even to the backyard,
or to sit in the rocker on the porch
before she enclosed it.
She had had an unnecessary mastectomy
and self-consciously stuffed the breast.
Her manner was so
no-nonsense and fierce
that she frightened most of my friends.
When Grandfather brought home the groceries
there was often something wrong:
"Only eleven oranges! You big boob! Can't you count?"

Once I remember Grandpa and I came back
from a trip to visit relatives in southeastern Ohio.
Grandpa went to her as she was washing the dishes,
and muttering softly "I missed you, Rose", bent
to give her a peck on the cheek.
She wheeled around, "Get out of here, Lou,
You bother me!" How often I wondered
how did they ever have children.
It seemed to me so inconceivable.
She never wanted her children to leave her,
and indeed they spent most of their lives
living with her
until she died.
Grandpa, ten years older, went first,
She covered his coffin and bedecked the whole parlor
with red gladiolas, Grandpa's favorite flower.
When he was gone we all noticed the change:
her manner was sweeter and kinder.

But when she died, all arrangements
had been made in advance:
no funeral, cremation, her ashes
to be tossed close to her childhood home
into the nearby Ohio River.
So Grandpa's big body decayed all alone
in the East Akron Cemetery.
There was no physical reason to account for her death.
Her heart was strong, said the doctor.
But how often she'd said, "This is no kind of life"—
"to live in a city bumped up to your neighbors,"
"to live a half-invalid" after she got
scoliosis at eighty.
She had such strength of mind that I think that she willed
her own death. My uncle said,
"She died mad." He sobbed
a whole year in his grieving.
My four-year-old daughter wistfully said
in a soft, solemn wonder,
"The little old granny is gone."
After my uncle's death, her ashes were found
in a cardboard box in a corner
covered with dust.
I took the box down to her childhood town
and threw the box in
to the flowing brown water.

Mailman Song

Bring me the mail, my uncle,
the letters that make my heart glad.
Bring me those bright picture postcards
from the best friend I ever had.

All of that love in your mailbag
stamped with encouraging words
for my weary and beat-up sad spirit
from the best friend I ever had.

Bring me the mail, dear Uncle,
each little halo of light,
a feather to fly to the sunshine,
a candle lit in the dark night.

Bring me the mail, my uncle,
poetry, prints, magazines,
museum bulletins, parcels,
art books, memories, dreams.

Bring me the mail, dear Uncle,
I never really guessed how you cared;
always sending me gifts and packages
from the best friend I ever had.

A Statue Of Saint Francis

By a statue of Saint Francis in a garden
    behind a Catholic church I'm seated weeping
on a stone bench beside a friend who tries in vain
    to comfort me in my loss, misunderstanding
my loss as it is not the loss she thinks is for
    a loving husband who has left me for another.
No, the loss is of a marriage that never was,
    and the loving husband promised that did not happen
except in precious minutes that would be hidden
    by hours of a harsher reality.

The stone-carved birds that sit on the saint's shoulder
    and are cradled in his hands express the freeze
of feelings that could have flown had they been living
    and not shot down by constant incivility.
Where was the passion and romance? 'Twas not to be.
    Alas for me I would become the butt
of jokes so clever I laughed hysterically
    as if I were too blind to even see
how much he had humiliated me.

At the first he had recalled to mind a painting
    of Saint Francis by El Greco I had loved
because he always wore a hooded jacket
    made of brown corduroy that wrapped his figure
which was slender and elongated like the image
    with a rosary made from a knotted rope,
knots that twisted me to endure three decades
    in madness, overeating, and misery
to hold onto a marriage emotionally as empty
    as his Franciscan vow of chastity.

And yet, and yet, how could I so forget
    the frames and breadboards and blanket chests
and wood panels he made for me to paint and
    our children that he gave who have so loved me.

Piano (Soft)
In Memory Of My Mother

Softly she fell asleep
for the last time in her life.
Sweetly she dimpled her cheeks
in her last smile,
and left this place a quiet peace,
a moment's grace in a world's strife.
I adored her from birth
for her soft pretty face
was framed with dark hair
in waves bobbed in the style
of Disney's Snow White.
She was blessed with brown eyes
fringed with long lashes,
which looked to me
the most beautiful on earth.
I remember her seated
at our parlor piano
playing the Paderewski minuet,
her pretty fingers dancing
like the French country dancers
printed white on her turquoise skirt
miming the motion
with the ribbons and lace
of her white eyelet blouse
as she played.
This piece was her favorite
and many years after
the piano was sold,
I heard it on the radio
driving down to DC,
and my tears couldn't stop
even after I got there.

Another favorite was
"September Song"
because she was born in September,
but her spirit was the month of May,
and her soul was St. Valentine's Day.

She could charm everyone
especially the menfolk,
and her artistic eye
and talented hands
made beautiful all
she touched.
Her sweet prettiness lingered
and clung to her being
even in the winter of old age.
So generous she was
for giving made her feel rich,
and she gave and gave and gave so much.
And I grieve because her life was hard,
and it should not have been,
and many did her wrong,
used her and abused her,
worst was her husband and her son.
She pretended not to mind
when people were cruel or unkind.
"There will be five stars
in my crown" she once told me.
But the stars in her crown
will outnumber the petals
that fall from magnolias
and dogwoods each spring,
or the sun's rays that sparkle
the teal ocean's waves,
and most of what's lovely
in my plain self she gave
like God's gift of His son
and the souls Jesus saves.

CALCULUS SONNETS

from ONE HUNDRED SONNETS TO THE CALCULUS

I. The Gift Of A Text
Full Of Errors

"What math gives students is certainty"

—Yoram Sagher

We don't have to pay to buy this text
because we'll pay in other ways, in loss
of trust and faith, confused, puzzled, perplexed,
unsure of answers when the answers given

are incorrect, so that the muddled mess
becomes a mystery of hell and heaven,
a passion play of curves and tangents flexed
to solve by finding limits to counteract

the gift of a family full of errors, yes,
and the gift of a world full of errors, tares
sown among the grain and cut en masse
as the text is grasped by mind and heart that cares

to differentiate the curves of fate
and integrate the love beneath the hate.

IV. The Removable Discontinuity

A tiny circle interrupts the line.
A value makes the fraction undefined.
It is the missing data and the sign

that leads us to the subtlety of form
God serves us in His riddled arrows firm
pointing to the little holes "forlorn"—

the very word that like a bell called Keats
to pour into his urn of metric beats
the sweat beads on his fevered body's heat.

The Spirit comes, called, desired, or unbidden
to close the discontinuity, the hidden
hole in the whole lifeline. The soul smitten

yearns to remove discontinuities, though hard
for what is impossible is possible with God.

VIII. Rules Of Power, Polynomial, Product, And Quotient

We can't forget the chain, the chain of minds
around the globe studying Calculus.
Newton and Leibniz live and that reminds
how history lives in the retelling to us.

All knowledge is not historical, Croce.
The bounds of senses, reason, accepted wisdom,
omit that which confounds, a piercing eye
of God whose intersection shows the kingdom.

The world we think is real and rely
steadfastly on becomes as just the smoke
spent from the crematory pyre. We fly,
new wings released, sprung from the mental yoke

by power rules that make the burdens light
like easy slumbers of a summer's night.

XXVI. Area Between Two Curves: Walking On Water At The Volo Bog

To compute the area of the pond in the bog,
first find the functions that shape the edge,
then use the definite integral, co-ordinates to log
what function to subtract between to gauge

the area of wood to step on above the sog-
gy peat that slowly sinks beneath the ledge
of styrofoam so as to walk in fog
on water from the past above the sinking sedge

with eyes upon a vision seen through smog
in winds that chill the feet with despair's sledge
driving down who stands in doubt. But jog
in faith through tamaracks that hedge

the area inside the bog, then God
with arms of curves joins two stakes that nod.

XXXVII. Proofs Of The Limit Laws

If given an egg of epsilon that's more
Than zero and a delta greater too,
So zero is less than the absolute
Value does imply that the Big Fix

Upon the cross is less than epsilon
For eggshells suffer badly stones and sticks,
And even for an eggshell Hamlet groaned
Soliloquizing at the frenzied fates

Our destinies and visions drive us to
Take arms against a sea of hiding hell,
And by opposing dive a drowning fool,
And O Horatio, what I could tell

Of limit less than let it break and be;
Not boiled enough, the yoke swims silently.

XLIII. The Chain Rule

To derive a function that fits inside another
function is to derive the outer function first
and multiply that times the inner one
and again for each more inside function

until the inmost inner is derived.
The global is the outermost, the size
of all human societies alive,
containing nations that contain the ties

of ethnic groups, political collections,
religions, towns, and families, each one
derived to find the tangents' touch, connections
to clasp the heart's concentric will to come

in time before the guns go off, bombs dropped.
The rule is first the world, the hating stopped.

XLV. Derivatives Of Sines And Cosines

How well they go together; how they change
into each other when derived again and again
with higher and higher derivation. True

love couldn't be more empathetic to do
such exchanging and role reversal, to descend
even to negatives as the derivations range

to higher powers. Would that we in others' shoes
could so see ourselves as the soul ascends
in this turning, burning, spiraling arranger

of divine rebirth. Like two sides of a coin,
like day and night, joy and sorrow, the change
of seasons, the tides, rotations that never end.

God's eternal love cycles the Son,
the circle sines and cosines square to one.

LXIV. The Derivative Of The Cross To An Irrational Power

The cross raised to a power equals e
Raised to that same power times the natural log
Of the cross so that when the derivative d
Over dx of the cross is taken, we leapfrog

To the e version, and get the power times
The cross raised to the power minus one.
This is done for the cross that cyclic comes
To irrationally derive to paradise a bum.

I read your latest book, Bill Matthews, wooing
Me with poems of *A Happy Childhood* to question,
"Hey, what's a fragile flower like you doing
With these torturing, bisecting mathematicians?

O come back to the poets, red rose-petaled hand;
We're the only ones who really understand."

LXX. Harmonic Oscillation And The Vibration Of Strings

The second derivative of the bow across
the violin strings added to the square
of the end omega crosses to equal the whole

note that looks like zero or an excited "O!"
Will this mathematical notation gloss
in harmony the heartstrings' song of care?

Will it play in Peoria or anywhere?
Will it play where dogwood blossoms toss
their petals to the winds of time, the toll

of the omega of vibration in the soul
of snapped synapses? Will it play there?
Or is it only to record and note the loss

of motion as it harmonically recedes
the shore the ocean rhythmically rereads.

LXXV. Integration By Parts—
When Simple Integration Fails,
Try This Formula

*"You were vain and vicious as we all are who craftily devise
the words to dance on empty graves."*

—Chad Walsh, "On Reading Thompson's
Biography of Robert Frost

A Novgorodian Virgin of Vladimir
Icon contains small versions of other icons:
Trinity, Harrowing of Hell, Forerunner.

When the tongue's touch, personal, poetic
turns to skull and crossbones, biting, acidic
with a press and pour of pain come chronic,

so words without love and comfort springing
only add poison to the stab and stinging;
memorized formulas come bringing

the way of integration, a healing answer:
Take the derivation of the product, ponder
a shift in the equation, integrate the sunder

by parts. Or memorize the formula, the food:
God's good, you are accepted, the past's approved.

LXXVIII. Infinite Series As A Circle Between Two Facing Mirrors

Chardin saw evolution as a series
of diversifying species until a stage
of maximum proliferation; species
would then begin extinction and converge

ultimately becoming but one species
of Christ consciousness. The edge
or turn from this diverging to converge
was like a globe with alpha one-celled species

at the southern pole and most diversely
evolved at the equator. Life forms would then
begin converging into a form like men
but rising to a spiritual supreme

he called omega, a planet's northern pole
where all of life transfigures into soul.

XCII. The Loss Of A Particular Constant When Reversing: Power Rule For Derivatives And Antiderivatives

You can't go home again without a loss.
What once was clear, specific, and well-known
drops into mystery like milk in sauce.
You can't go back and get the milk alone,

or know it is not butter, flour, cheese,
but one of these, and so we mark it C,
or K if you are German, if you please.
It is a constant unspecifically.

If you translate this sonnet into French,
then back to English, you will see that words
have several synonyms whose meanings drench
with subtle changes, and the choice is blurred.

Going home you recognize the place,
but something's not the same in what you face.

XCVIII. The Bridge Linking Differentiation And Integration: The Fundamental Theorem Of Calculus

This gives to you two constants j and k,
with a continuous function in between,
like a suspension bridge is a grand way
connecting two communities and seen

to be a link rising across a strait
or a river like the Brooklyn Bridge, which spans
the Hudson, or the bridge called Golden Gate.
It's a sparkling clarity that stands and brands

into the brain this fundamental tie
that binds our hearts even if we divide
as differential parts that dumbly try
to break the spirit-bond that tender hides
and whispers of the fundamental truth
that we are all connected deep inside.

C. Blowing Kisses To Ron Coleman At The Kelvyn Park High School Retirement Dinner, June, 2008

A tragic loss of sight keeps Ron at home,
and so he is not present here for us.
He who has given much and then excess
of much I know would greatly wish to come.

Well, I am here to honor this great man,
but can I make this sonnet integral,
a slice to fully measure all in all,
the volume of that vast accomplished sum?

It is too hard. My geometric, very
limited poetic skills too dear
to see the way God sees that Ron is here,
the way the number *i*, imaginary,

raised to an even power becomes the real
man in us we love and deeply feel.

SONNETS TO THE PSALMS

from SONNETS TO THE PSALMS

Sonnets 1

"like a tree planted by the rivers of water"

—Psalms 1: 3a

So many do not understand
how desperately we need the trees.
They burn them down to clear the land
nor heed the warnings of a few-degrees-

hotter yearly temperatures or pleas
to save the habitat of birds and fish
that vanish to extinction when trees vanish.
Aren't trees but our front lines against the desert?

Trees make the oxygen we breathe to live.
Trees shield from wind and rain and blazing skies.
Trees hold the moisture that would vaporize
away and dry the soil that would erode and give

the land to gullies and advancing dunes.
Without the trees, the earth's a barren moon.

I do not like you, Mr. T.
Your new wealth bought a forested estate,
but you would not keep a single tree.
You shocked your neighbors to an angry hate.

They tried to get the law to stop your saws.
Those trees had stood for centuries; now fate
for money put their lives within your claws.
Why does the great Sahara increase in Africa?

For trees don't grow on money but on years;
ring after ring their trunks record the rounds
they've used in reaching upwards. How it spears
my heart to see you speedily cut them down!

Time will remember this when you are old.
No shelter is in hell for squandered gold.

I do not like you, nation of Brazil.
Your tropical rainforests grow
on unexpectedly unfertile soil
where shallow-rooted soaring palms and ferns

are wrapped by thick lianas and orchid vines
and make an Eden for the jaguar. Your people burn
and the monkeys, plants, and toucans can't return.
Where are now the trees that drank the greenhouse gas?

They're burning into carbon and monoxide
to make room for farms that last a year or two
and abandoned for more burning to a waste as wide
as the Amazon River Blindness and as true

as planting one for ten cut down will tell
that planet earth warms to a burning hell.

When the Amazonian rainforests burn
and pump their tons of CO2 into
the over burdened atmosphere we learn
that not only seven billion trees and plants are gone

which would have gladly drunk a ton or two
of the yearly multiplying excess CO2
but exponentially the climate change raises the stakes.
Will Holland and Florida drown before we wake?

And will the Midwest grain fields die in drought
before enough people bother to figure out
what all the alarms and warnings are about,
and it's too late to grow the trees we need.

Those over fifty will die before that day,
but the younger ones will have to pay and pay.

Sonnet 26

"Gather not my soul with sinners,
nor my life with bloody men:
in whose hands is mischief . . ."

—Psalms 26: 9, 10a

Now may my dwelling be in quilts and poems,
in prayers and sacred songs. May I rise up
with sacred choirs singing all the morns
of all my life. And may I my home clean up
to be as fragrant as my flowers and trees that sup
the stormy rains. May all who think me warm
and open, an easy mark, a naïve dope,
be thwarted in their designs and cons, disarmed
divinely and transformed to thy cause and quest.
May communities be cleansed and full of song.
May all people pull together and give their best
to build a loving world where all belong,
comforted and healed and free of sin,
like quilts and poems and prayers and songs to Him.

Sonnet 32

*"When I kept silence, my bones waxed old
through my roaring all the day long."*

—Psalms 32: 3

Why can I never fully flush this shout
of outrage from within? Why does the anger
hang like a heavy anchor to stay my boat
and stop my sailing free? What stranger
stronger than any guide I've met, with clout
clearer and more pure than any danger
could push aside, can pull the weight that doubt
has dumped within me? The Christmas manger
shines only in the scripture; my prayer and praise
sound in a minor key too frazzled and unfit
for God's triumphant servant; the struggling days
too marred with demon wrestling, pushing pirates
overboard only to turn and face the cutlass teeth
clawing the side as sharks swim underneath.

Sonnets 42

"Deep calleth unto deep at the noise of thy waterspouts:
all thy waves and thy billows are gone over me."

—Psalms 42:7

Our life begins as fish in a womb-sized sea
much like the ancient sea from which fish crawled
upon the land where fish to man evolved.
This unkind kind with greatest brain won't see

how dead red tides from ocean dumping fouled
these living waters that fed him clean and free
once, these garbaged waters that now plea
with dying dolphins, poisoned shellfish culled

from deadly toxic bays and estuaries,
sea turtles choked on plastic bags and things
mistook for jellyfish, muzzled starved sea
lions with noses poked in nets and rings.

Fin rot, ulcers, holes burned in lobsters tell
of man-made chemicals in a man-made hell.

Dear God, is there a way to save the seas?
A way to stop the dumping and pollution?
A way to clean the bays and estuaries?
And keep them clean: What is your best solution?

Kill manunkind in a blazing retribution?
Or let him kill himself with PCB,
and the other toxic wastes in earth and ocean,
and then give back the earth to the lower species.

Let not this judgment fall so hard on man.
May your mercy fill his heart with loving care
for all your creatures. Make his ways so fair
that earth becomes the garden it began.

Wash up man's act before he's all washed up,
and global suicide's his poisoned cup.

Sonnets 45

"My tongue is the pen of a ready writer.
Thou art fairer than the children of men:
Grace is poured into thy lips."

—Psalms 45: 1c

Warm air invites washed clean with spring's new rain.
Purple and yellow crocus join the songs
of birds to bless my yearning breast again
with memories of country mornings long
ago in childhood. How fresh and sane
and pure was then the way to live! Gone
the chickens, pigs, haymow, the horses, grain,
the trees, the flowers, cornfields, the cows, all gone
with Uncle Joe, Aunt Estella, the farm. Now only
this fresh moist air returns me to that place
of youthful joy, more vividly, less lonely,
than ever reverie. Strange gift of nature's grace
to feel the dew with bare feet in wet grass,
to smell the hollyhocks and sassafras.

My brother, you too are gone. You and the swing
that seemed to hang from heaven and swung out
from the top of a sloping hill like a wooden wing
into the upper leaves of maples. Doubt,
despair had no place in that sunshine sling
up way over the hen coop where the roosters shout
and pullets peeuck-puck-puck, pick kernels, fling
white feathers as they fly the fence about.
The drop and feathers in the stomach as you climbed
higher in the air to where the trees caressed
your toes like leafy gods tickling five mimed
piggies: market, home, food, none, distressed,—
back down and up again unless you dropped
your feet, and digging dirt, their heels stopped.

Sonnet 91

"He shall cover thee with his feathers, and under his wings
shalt thou trust; his truth shall be thy shield and buckler."

—Psalms 91: 4

What's left of all the dinosaurs who thundered
bodacious bodies before the mammals came
in tiny horse and woolly mammoth herds?
The descendants of the dinosaurs became
the light and winged creatures we call birds.
From giant lizards we got loons, some claim,
and sparrows, owls, hawks, eagles, wrens, and songbirds,
flamingoes, turkeys, geese, evolved the same.
If brontosaurus whose fossils fill whole rooms
begot the hummingbird, why then what doom
is death? Extinction's evolution's sieve—
what of creation dies and what will live.
So earthly bodies sink like dinosaurs
their bones in bogs so their winged spirit soars.

Sonnet 96

"Let the field be joyful, and all that is therein: then shall all the trees of the wood rejoice before the LORD; for he cometh, for he cometh to judge the earth . . .

—*Psalms 96: 12*

Snow-frosted Douglas firs in silence stand,
forms softened by the fog's November morn.
Round the ancient trunks of sequoias grand,
the soul finds refuge from the chainsaw's groan.

When a young man, Paul Rokich, saddened, planned
beneath the desolate clear-cut Utah mountains
to make them green again. A hundred thousand
of acres with thousand thousands of trees are bird reborn.

So I plant acorns to give the oaks my hand,
and write the Senate to give the trees a horn
whose leaves but whisper to hearts that understand
our connections to the squirrels, oaks, and acorns.

Divine green spirit, help us plant and care
to reap a greener, more song-filled, clean-air year.

Sonnet 107

"He poureth contempt upon princes, . . . Yet setteth he
the poor on high from affliction, And maketh him families like
a flock."

—Psalms 107: 40, 41

There's never sufficient reason to despair.
Though dunces, scoundrels be voted to high office,
though poor and homeless huddle everywhere,
though hypocrisy and lies mask power's malice,
though dreams dissolve like sulfur in the air,
and rain their bitter disappointed dust
to acid etch the soul beyond repair,
though hard-won gains be trashed by cruel and callous
so-called public servants, yet every hair
is numbered, and each faint hope that hops
with lagomorphic life leaps Fred Astaire-
like dancing a delight of growing gallops.
A pitied, pecked, plucked bird can sing and fly
when God's love tunes the throat and strings the sky.

Sonnet 138

"Though I walk in the midst of trouble, thou wilt revive me: thou shalt stretch forth thine hand against the wrath of mine enemies, and thy right hand shall save me."

—Psalms 138: 7

Hard work and sacrifice are not enough.
The world today is too political.
Too many managers make tasks too tough.
They use the stress of no-win to enthrall
with power to enslave, make life so rough
that all suffer at their whim and maul,
and if you have the nerve to call their bluff
the nasty game it is, to have that gall,
then you will pay the bitter price, and God
alone can save you from their wrath. But yet
impotence can be the power of the odd,
and to walk away can mark you as a prophet.
The truest measure of a man of power
is how he treats those under: do they flower?

Sonnet 139

"Whither shall I go from thy spirit? Whither shall I flee from thy presence? If I ascend up into heaven thou art there. If I make my bed in hell, behold, thou art there. If I say, surely the darkness shall cover me, even the night shall be made light about me . . . the darkness and the light are both alike to thee."

—Psalms 139: 7, 8, 11, 12c

In the beginning light and dark were good,
like yin and yang, two parts to make a whole,
for each defined the other as contrast should.

And when did dark become the evil dole?
A function of the fall from innocence?
Redemption then restores dark's rightful role.

The quilt Sunshine and Shadow represents
that all is good when love is in control
and fills its artful place in immanence.

A white dove and a black swan paint your soul,
rainbows of birds and flowers, colors that laud
creation's gift; joys light and dark unroll.

With love His Son for us survived the rod,
so no dark cliff, white wall keeps us from God.

Sonnet 150

"Praise him with the sound of a trumpet . . . psaltery and harp . . . string instruments and organs . . . Praise ye the Lord."

—Psalms 150: 3, 4b. 6b

Around us moves an unseen lace of love
Most vivid in our childhood's wondering awe
When hearts are small and soft as a kitten's paw,
What most people have but a memory of.
Around us hums this harmony of love
Unheard amidst the traffic and the noise
That hurts our ears and blasts away our joys,
But it can cover like a furry glove
If we but still our mind and empty be
Like woodwinds waiting for a blowing burst
That starts the skillful touch so much rehearsed,
That bows the strings and presses piano keys
To release the singing voice that praising swells
And moves the hands that shake the ringing bells.

POEMS ON THE TWENTY-THIRD PSALM

from ANOINTING MY HEAD WITH SINGING ALL THE DAYS OF MY LIFE:
FIFTEEN POEMS ON THE TWENTY-THIRD PSALM

The Black Lamb

"The Lord is my shepherd"

Little black lamb, little black lamb,
Bleating by that old trashcan,
Oh, I know it's not so pretty
In this poor part of the city.

Your momma's going to have another.
Will he be lamb chops like your brother?
And your daddy's in the pen.
Who knows when you'll see him again.

But you've a daddy in the sky.
He was a lamb come down to die.
With black wool we called him Martin.
Oh, he loves you, that's for certain.

Little black lamb, little black lamb,
Live your life as best you can.
Black is beautiful, not man,
And your good shepherd is a lamb.

Carol Of The Colors

"I shall not want"

If Christ is born in all that lives,
He'll not depart from one who loves.

If Christ is born in every day,
In every heart, to all who pray,
Then He will come and He will stay,
And not depart from one who loves.

The angels call on rainbow wings,
Singing "Rejoice!", glad tidings bring;
In every voice an angel sings
If Christ is born in all that lives.

When morning breaks, the angel's rose;
The angel's orange when sunlight glows;
The angel's gold in noon's bright clothes
If Christ is born in all that lives.

In azure sky, the angel's blue;
In sunset's shade, a purple hue;
In grass and trees, a green dressed view
If Christ is born in all that lives.

For when the sun goes down to bed,
The angel's wine, the angel's red;
The angel's black with starry head
If Christ is born in all that lives.

If Christ is born in every day,
In every heart, to all who pray,
Then He will come and He will stay,
And not depart from one who loves.

I Am My Own
Best Company

"He maketh me to lie down in green pastures"

In truth I am my own best company.
The Christ that lives within sustains and heals.
Although I live alone, I am not lonely.

There is no friend as kind and full of mercy
Who sees so clearly and knows just how it feels.
In truth I am my own best company.

People entreat and take until I'm empty;
Put me aside to find another meal;
Although I live alone, I am not lonely.

Though out to pasture, I view contently
A nature TV show about a seal.
In truth I am my own best company.

I've piles of fabric so I can sew so many
Quilts to please and comfort, give and feel.
Although I live alone, I am not lonely.

I know my life is good though elderly;
The journey's real, and memories reveal
The truth that I'm my own best company,
And though I live alone, I am not lonely.

Olive Variations

"Thou anointest my head with oil"

Here is a jar of green olives
with their bloody pimento tongues,
the green a gold ochre olive,
the juice wedding water and oil.

Here is a small can of tuna,
imported from Italy tonno,
fish flakes of pink drenched in olive
oil wedding water and juice.

Here is a plate of spaghetti
sauced with tomato and meat,
garlic, oregano, onion,
water wedding oil and juice.

Here is an old Popeye cartoon.
When Bluto carts off "me Olive!"
the sailor pops up his spinach
juice wedding Oyl and ocean.

Here is an account of how Jesus
ascended into heaven in a cloud
from Mt. Olivet full of olives,
oil wedding water into wine.

Thanksgiving Haiku

"My cup runneth over."

A blue china cup
a child left out in the rain
fills and overflows.

Cold November day,
grey coat caught by bare branches,
my eyes flow with tears.

Packed into a box
with roast turkey, dressing,
the gravy boat spills.

A Thanksgiving feast
with pecan pumpkin pie leaves
lots of leftovers.

I turn on the tap.
The water rinsing my cup
freely runs over.

NATURE
AND
ENVIRONMENT

Sonnet In Early May

The trap is set for the skunk beneath my deck
among the garbage cans in my backyard,
but it's spring for an old woman and this hard
reality is softened with the scent

of apple blossoms and words seemed sent
from angel lips. How sweet the kind reward!
The limbs are thick with blossoms opened toward
the few bees busy at the nectar meant

just for them to move from tree to tree
to pollinate so petals fall to apples
starting green and small and dappled
ripening red and speckled to drop free

like the blowing gentle petals if I wait
rocking on the glider near the gate.

Earthworm

My lacy castings lay
     like copper coins
to give my lair away
     where tunnel joins
the air for robins prey
     and pull my loins
     in easy slide
on this earth's muddy clay
     amusement ride.

Under The Magnolia

I have come to my daughter's house to see
her huge old flowering magnolia tree.
She is not home, but a memory
leads me to stand under the canopy
of white and magenta bevies of bloom.
I remember a child in a once-sunny noon
sleeping under a blanket of magnolia flowers.
I painted that picture though I could not now tell
what happened to it, so I could not now show
what it looked like. It is just as well.
I don't remember she liked it. So only I see
that painting of my daughter asleep in a sea
floating in petals of pale pink ivory
sweet-scented magenta veined with burgundy.

In The Glory Of
The Morning

The morning glories twine azure and wine
flared trumpets on the many-stemmed vine
through silvered steel links that fence away
the neighbor's yard and dogs. The dawning day
lights up the links electric in the sun;
the flowers sparkle with metallic spun
radiance and halos. Struck with the sight
I pause and welcome in the joy of light.
O that such beauties suddenly amaze
my eyes and heart despite my hectic days
and mounting worries, cares, is spiritual grace
to lift and lighten like a loving face,
a hallowed space of feeling, an awesome swell
of music from the realm where all is well.

The Golden Swan

A white swan glides across the lake
shining in the dazzling sun drops
as the sun descends in a late afternoon
like a white boat heaped with gold
doubloons, caskets, and snake-necked urns.

This golden avatar of yellow sunbeams
caressing shadows that peek beneath the waves
as I gaze intently instantly takes flight
straight toward that blinding source of light
dissolving into pixels, blurring to my sight,
to vanish in a sun of yellow roses.

This June

Has been an alternating monsoon;
storm follows sun follows storm follows sun,
a metronome of unusual weather
like a traffic light signals stop and go,
the heartbeat's pulses and pauses,
the continuing cosine graph of the tides,
the swinging pendulum of a clock,
and the song of the lungs.
I'm thanking God for it
like a sinner reborn.
I do not have to water the flowers.

Ode To A Snowflake

I

In truth, I've traced your form so crystalline
With wire and beads, with scissors and cut paper,
With fabric appliquéd your wee design

Exploded many magnitudes, the shaper
Of the magnifying glass's work.
I watch you swirl, whirl, blow, and caper,

Free and cold upon my nose and cheeks.
I catch you on my tongue like a raindrop,
And on my lashes' tips a weeping creek

Beneath the jeweled crystals of its top,
Which finds its own path in a trickling flow,
Hid from the wintry blast and icy pop.

A song to you, O tinker bell of snow!
O teeny star within a milky way,
Against the night I see your tiny glow

Amid a million like you swirling away,
Hexagonal geometry of time
That melts to vapor like a dot of day.

II

For shoveling up ten inches of your kin
To clear my sidewalk and dig out my car,
Lovely snowflake, more than did me in.

And can I still remember you're a star
And in the freezing wind and snow's wet bluster
Find inspiration for my soul's guitar?

For even in your freshly fallen luster
You sparkle when the icy cold wind jars
Our shivers and shakes down a snowy cluster.

But when the thawing sun and passing cars
Melt your heavy mounds with peppered soot,
We go to the ice show to see the stars

Whirling, swirling, spinning on one foot
Or in the air with awesome twirling leaps
With grace and skill and energy output.

For though the ice might be few inches deep,
The metal of the skates crisscrossing scars
Spray the glistening flakes in gentle sweeps.

III

O cold wet symbol of God's lovely chill
That comes along with death's deep darkening channel
Swirling to a comfort zone of care
With Christ our Lord who suffered, died, and fell
Into a tomb of dark and dismal tunnel
To wake and take us shining in the air.

Don't Overlook
The Unexpected

While you travel life's interstate,
pay close attention
to love's little gestures:
the slender vase of fresh flowers
between shiny basins
in the turnpike restroom.
Forget what you've seen in the toilets.
Flush all that away.
Remember, rejoice
in the red carnations
and the white baby's breath
in the milk-glass vase
on the counter
where you washed your hands.

Global Warning

A certain tree needs a fungus near to grow.
　　Smart bees cross-pollinate.
Dumb bees stay in one tree to blow the show
　　and make the fruit third-rate.
Life is limited more ways than we can know.

The strangler fig and Spanish moss drape hosts
　　long after they have died.
And kudzu carpets woods to shape green ghosts
　　of the dying trees inside.
Nature's revenge on man's mistaken boasts
　　is a man-poisoned tide.
If we don't become fit husband to earth-wife,
we'll make the earth unfit for any life.

He Goes Where
Rubber Flows

The rubber drips from two cuts in the trunk,
    But only two, no more,
For more would turn the golden goose to skunk
    And empty out the drawer
for milky liquid latex rivers sunk

In chevron scars of past years' gatherings.
    Macaws and toucans call the name
of Chico Mendes; all the rainforest sings.
    Now cattle all are lame
with hoof and mouth, malaria sweeps clearings
    when plants are all the same.
They torched a forest's wealth and found poor lands.
They murdered Mendes for saving rubberbands.

Plant A Tree

To save the earth from sun and sea
from monoxide buildup and desert drought
go out today and plant a tree.

The trees are cut and burned down globally
at a rate of ten to one seedling's sprout
which will flood the earth with sun and sea

eventually.

At that rate, Miami and Washington DC,
better build those dikes high and stout
or go out today and plant a tree,

or two or more like ten billion three
for the earth's heating up and time's running out
to save the earth from sun and sea.

Plant an apple, a maple, a spruce, oak, or cherry,
a bamboo, a palm, gum, banyan, or loquat;
go out today and plant a tree.

Make it cool and green for posterity
or move to Alaska if you doubt
we can save the earth from sun and sea

because people are so careless, blind, and greedy,
and don't know what's happening and won't find out
that to save the earth from sun and sea,
we all need to go out and plant a tree.

Dream Trees

Somewhere in a deserted valley
I am planting trees
from the seeds of criterion apples
and the acorns of white oaks,
from the wings of sugar maples,
the keys of ashes, and Indian beans of catalpas,
the stones of flowering cherries,
dogwoods, crabapples, peaches, pears.
Somewhere on the banks of streams
I am planting bald cypresses and red maples,
dawn redwoods, magnolias, crape myrtles.
Somewhere I am planting trees,
Firs, pines, and spruces in my dreams,
and even here, although
many there are who do not love a tree.
They cut it down to build a town
with hot and dusty streets,
and sunbaked office buildings,
houses and apartments air-conditioned
expensively and heated expensively
in winter. Many there are
who think they have no need of trees,
who tear down branches and trample seedlings,
who poison and bury tree roots,
and deny a tree a drink of water
in a drought. Many more than those who care
and love ecstatically the trees
for all their beautiful seasons,
their protective cooling shade,
and fruits for the birds and wildlife.

When the trees are gone,
and the birds and animals are gone,
what then will the chainsaws cut?
When I die the trees will receive me.
They will draw me up through their roots
and into their leafy arms,
where my soul will perch and sing,
or flutter like a moth in the breeze,
or hoot like an owl in the moonlight.
I will be dew on their flowering parts;
I will sink deep into their flowers and fruits,
and I will live again with every tree that sprouts,
and every dream of trees.

STRAWBERRY VARIATIONS

I. Alexi's Strawberries

Baby Alexi has a big strawberry
birthmark on her cheek.
It will grow small
till it's hardly at all
as Alexi learns how to speak.

Baby Alexi has a small strawberry
heart shape on her arm.
So sweet to the eyes,
if it stays the same size,
Really now, what is the harm?

The angels come down when no one's around
and baby is fast asleep.
So many soft kisses,
dreams and dear wishes
on her strawberries red they heap.

II. Strawberry Roan

Let's go for a ride on a strawberry roan.
Over fields we'll glide and leap over stone
to search for the leprechauns' hidden zone
deep in the side of a mountain's moan.

We'll go for a ride on a strawberry roan,
only stars to guide and the wind to groan,
to skip in the tide where the white gulls drone,
forever together and never alone.

III. *Fragaria Virginiana Of The Rose Family*

I'm stringing strawberries
  in groups of Hail Mary's
   for a rosary spaced with plums
between for Our Father's,
  the prayer Christ taught us
   to say as we move our thumbs.

The strange fact the strawberry
  is not really a berry
   or a fruit not everyone knows.
Because the small flowers
  are ringed by five sepals,
   the strawberry's really a rose.

IV. The Sharpening Strawberry

At my feet on the rugs my son
had piled up in the stairwell,
there lay a large needle-and-pin-
sharpening strawberry.

The looped green cord not torn
at the top clearly was not pulled
from a tomato cushion for pins.
Perhaps it dropped unseen
at my feet

when I had carried upstairs
some of grandmother's quilts.
It will in this silence sharpen my wits
to think to mend with grains of metal
(mettle?) my threads torn from unseen
hands that placed it so poetically
at my feet.

V. What's Left For Darryl Strawberry?

(The Underachievin' Blues)

Oh, I came up like lightnin'
Winnin' Rookie of the Year.
Oh, I came up like lightnin',
And how the fans did cheer.

I slugged two hundred homers
Sooner than any other star.
I slugged two hundred homers.
Cooperstown weren't dat far.

They paid me lotsa millions,
But I was lazy chasin' balls.
They paid me lotsa millions,
But I exercised my jaws.

My record ain't so good no more,
And my bat ain't so hot.
My record ain't so good no more,
Ain't behavin' like I ought.

I hit my wife and pulled a gun,
Was havin' babes by other women.
I hit my wife and pulled a gun,
Drinkin', druggin', sinnin'.

But I found Christ in '91;
No more shrinks abidin'.
Yeah, I found Christ in '91,
But now I am backslidin'

Woe is me, what's to be done?
My glory years are gone now.
Woe is me, what's to be done?
My time to shine is gone now.

Bovine Beauties

#1 Rosie O'Grady And Peggy O'Neil

Were two Jersey heifers
born on St. Patrick's Day,
so Uncle Joe gave them Irish names
and touched them in a special way.
They gave more milk and richer cream
than all his other cows.
They moo and sway now in a dream
while agribusiness house
bovines numbered consecutively
lined up in hundreds, thousands.
Machines feed grain and pull the udders;
no human strokes with human hands,
no human names, no loving mutters.
You think those cows don't understand?
Mad cow disease invades the land.

#2 The Geometry Of Circles In Marc Chagall's Painting I And The Village

A dark man's profile stares at a cow's light head.
The white eye of this blind man sights a thread,
A chord connecting to the cow's dark eye.
The man's hand offers to the cow what I
Would call a sprig of heart-shaped leaves and fruit
To link the man's mouth to the cow's babe-cute
Muzzle that makes a circle cut in wedges
Like a pizza aligning both their noses' edges.
A reaper with a woman upside down
Walks up the hill curved between two crowns.
The cow's cheek is tattooed with a maid who milks
A cow left-handed and her right hand holds in back
A deep-red rose. The cow and man are stringed
With beads about their necks; his finger's ringed.

#3 A Seuss Mulberry Street Memory Of The Summer Of Chicago's Cow Parade

Art for everyone
Bright colored paint
In glorious design
All up and down
Michigan Avenue.
Poetry for everyone
Metaphors and puns
Alliteration and assonance
Fantasy and rhyme
And a swell of a time
All up and down Michigan.
Cows atop skyscrapers
Cows on the streets
Cows on sightseeing boats
Cows in the windows
Cows on the sidewalks
Cows on the grass
Cameras clicking
At kids sitting on cows
And adults kissing cows.
Movie-star cows
Midnight cows
With constellations of stars
And moon-jumping cows
Rembrandt, Da Vinci, Rafael cows
Venus de Moolo
And impressionist cows
Pointillist and cubist cows
Abstract and surreal cows
Picowso, Moonet
Van Cowgh and Cowquin
Moolouse Cowtrec
of the Moolin Mooge
Mooving cows, mooning cows

Shaken not steered cows
Brown cows, purple cows
Royal cows, Viking cows
Salt of the earth and everyman cows
Dressed-to-the-nines cows
Cows in hats and cows in bloomers
Renaissance-costumed cows
"Moo-moo in a tutu" ballerina cows
Egyptian cows
Ethiopian cows
Jewish cows and Irish cows
French cows and Polish cows
Romantic cows and Blues cows
Nursery rhyme and storybook cows
Calculator and computer cows
Sitting cows and dancing cows
Standing cows and walking cows
Heads-down and heads-up cows
Clown cows and tragic cows
Statue of Liberty and Twin Towers cows
All up and down
Michigan Avenue
And into the side streets
And onto the river
Around and around
The Loop and the town
Walking, dancing, lying down
A Hallelujah herd of Holy Cows
Color splashed
Dream dashed
Wonder washed
Rainbow hued
Sunshine sparkled
Love-in symphony
Creative celebration
Of cows.

#4 The Milk Of Human Kindness

Heaven sent are the cows of our spirits.
Our heavenly farmer milks our souls,
Leads us to His heavenly pastures,
Yoked invisibly together.

Come, let us be kind to one another,
Open our milk cartons of love and pour
Wisely abundant to all.

#5 Was There A Cow In The Stable

Was there a cow in the stable, even one?
Only Luke tells the tale, and he doesn't say.
Was there a cow at the birth of God's Son?

The journey had been long, and the supper was done.
The inn was overcrowded, and where could they stay?
Was there a cow in the stable, even one?

One look at Mary, and the innkeeper, stunned,
Knew in his heart he could not turn them away.
Was there a cow at the birth of God's Son?

Sheep, goats, a rooster to crow with the sun?
What animals were there in the straw on that day?
Was there a cow in the stable, even one?

There's no way to know it for certain, none,
But I'd like to believe near where Jesus lay
That there was a cow at the birth of God's Son,

A cow licking the baby's feet with her tongue
When Mary bore Jesus and laid Him in the hay.
I say there was a cow in the stable, even one,
I say there was a cow at the birth of God's Son.

PARODIES

The Ballad Of The Bobbitts

To be sung to the tune of "Frankie and Johnny"

Lorena and Johnny were lovers;
at least that's how it began.
She was his third-world woman,
and he made her an American.
He was her man, but the loving went wrong.

John was always pushing for coupling,
as often as the trains go through.
John had a more active organ
than E. Power Biggs ever knew.
He was her man, but he was coming on too strong.

A woman needs some special attention.
A woman needs some time and space.
A woman needs a man who won't shove his
you-know-what always in her face.
He was her man, but she's no Erica Jong.

Lorena tried to tell him to slow down.
She tried just saying NO.
But what she got were hurts and bruises
in places that didn't show.
He was her man, but he was treating her wrong.

John Wayne's a powerful moniker,
and it's curious where it's been found.
There's a John Wayne awaiting execution,
who kept thirty corpses around.
He was her man, but he was looking like King Kong.

Lorena tried to be a good woman,
so she could be an American wife,
but was it anger or an insane impulse
that led her to reach for that knife?
He was her man, but she sure did him wrong.

This story is sad, but it's funny,
for those who saw his thing land,
packed it away in ice cubes
for the surgeon's skillful hand.
He was her man, and it's back where it belongs.

It's hard to prove rape in marriage,
emotional and physical abuse;
when you've severed your husband's penis,
you've put your own neck in the noose.
He was her man, but she sure bobbed it wrong.

So John was found innocent of abusing;
Lorena was found temporarily insane.
The juries felt they'd tortured each other
so much there was no more need for blame.
He was her man, but the loving went wrong.

The moral of this story,
The moral of the Bobbitts' case
is the forgiveness of both those juries
deepens John's and Lorena's disgrace.
Who'll be her man? And that's the end of this song.

I Won't Have Sex With You In Buckingham Fountain

Because even though my husband left me
to wed another,
he still lives.
Because even though you asked me to go to the Dells
with you over spring break,
you didn't care.
Because we are not married and shouldn't have sex
even in a private place.
Because even if no one appears to be around to see
we could be arrested, and
Because the water is too cold.

The Dove

(In response to Edgar Allan Poe's "The Raven)

Now as it's but five-thirty just before the dawn is flirty
I take my pen and paper to record what will occur.
After I've prayed repeating for each bead and entreating
supplications for the needy, I hear a gentle stir.
"Tis a message," soft I murmured, "muffled quiet like a purr,
                a fluff of feathers or of fur."

As I sit here broken-hearted thinking back just how it started,
I meditate in wonder his electrical allure;
how it set me spinning boldly but to have it ending coldly,
still the silence as we parted piercing my heart like a spur
from his charismatic charm and crazy animated whirr,
                nameless here as only "sir".

Beset with joyful visions that may prove but vain illusions
filling me with fresh confusions so the present is a blur
in the deep pain still returning, all my passions still are churning
while the pages I am turning of my Bible as it twere
a divining rod at random some wise guidance to procure
                to calm my grief for "sir."

My rosary confessing as the green beads I'm caressing
seeking an added blessing so that I may strong endure,
again I fell to dreaming such rich fantasies flew teeming,
so again I hear the murmur like a teasing fish-hooked lure
promising me magic miracles I know will not occur,
                reuniting me with "sir."

But again the gentle motion like a rubbing in of lotion
as though a blowing notion lifted up my hair above
my sweating scalp's hot ocean, pouring down its sticky potion
cooled astringently and loosely like a gelatin-soaked glove,
calmed caressingly and moistly like what the dew's made of,
                my dove's cooing "peace and love."

Ah, lullabies of benediction better than a work of fiction
to sweep me in convections with fond dreams that are filled of
heavenly resurrections and reassuring dictions
in voices of affections that murmuringly prove
soft whispers of inflections that musically move
                              my dove's cooing "peace and love."

God bless this comforting bird's cooing so like a lover wooing
mumbling prayerful refrains as though an angel strove
to keep my heart from straying to where the evil's laying
in wait to take me down below to wallow with the foe
preying on inexperience when praying makes shields of
                              my dove cooing "peace and love."

O gentle dove so softly singing, evoking distant cowbells ringing,
into my hands you're springing as a spirit from above.
As my fingers your feet clinging, I stroke your feathers winging
ruffled halos of white flinging, angelic clouds that I've dreamed of,
blessed with mercy bringing from heaven's kisses I've dreamed of,
                              ever cooing "peace and love."

To Edgar Allan Poe

As I walked by the lake in November
   Through the skeletal trees to the cries
Of the migrating geese to remember,
   Oh, remember this year as it dies!

As I wandered the shores of Lake Sunder
   Salving my heart with the lies
The mind weaves to bind the wounds tender
   From lost friends and many good-byes,

As I thought of my father and mother,
   One long in the grave and the ties
Tearing away from the other
   As soured milk curdles replies,

As I wearily stumbled, the thunder
   Brought down the cold drops from the skies
Pounding my face in fierce anger
   To squeeze in and wring out my eyes.

Then I mused that your life was much stranger
   Than the usual lows and the highs,
The weather foreboding of danger
   And the waves ebbing full of your sighs.

You Are Old, Mrs. Enright

A parody of "Father William" by Lewis Carroll

"You are old, Mrs. Enright,"
      my students said,
"and your hair has gone completely gray.
      You're weary and cross
      cause we're lazy and gross.
Why don't you retire today?"
"In my youth," said the senior,
      "I studied and scored
and soared high above all the others.
      Their envy and spite
      made it their delight
to persecute, harry, and trouble."

"You are old, Mrs. Enright,"
      my students said,
"and you've grown most uncommonly fat.
      Yet you raced round the room
      with a ruler and broom.
How did your large size manage that?"
"In my youth," said the dame,
      "I developed a game
for dancing suspended in air,
      and the agility gained
      has been my luck to remain
and cause sleepy students to stare."

"You are old, Mrs. Enright,"
      my students said,
"and your voice is loud, raspy, and hoarse.
      Yet you sing a soprano
       that floats a vibrato
as if an archangel sang for us."
"In my youth," said the crone,
      "as I walked my way home
past the rubber factories roaring in Akron,
      I bellowed each hymn
      way above all the din
as Christ can raise you," said the matron.

The Prayer Of The Gardener

Francis,
Make me a fiddle fern of your holy foolishness.
Where there are thistles, let me plant lettuce;
Where there is crabgrass, violets.
Where there are dandelions, let me plant clover;
Where there are brambles, blueberries.
Where there is ragweed, let me plant rhubarb;
Where there is goldenrod, yams.

O beloved saint, let me not look out
Only on my own garden,
But let me enjoy my neighbor's too.
Let me not eat up all my own vegetables,
But pass on some of them to food pantries.
Let me not only eat all my apples,
But pass them out on Halloween.
For it is in sharing our zucchinis,
That we get zucchini bread;
It is in handing out carrots, we get carrot cake;
And it is in pulling weeds
That we get space for growing tomatoes.

ART, PEOPLE, & MATH

Forget Mapplethorpe And "Consider The Lilies"

Entranced was I by a hibiscus's come-hither tongue,
A blowtorch of pollen and pistil to flagrantly spark
From trumpets of petticoat petals that rustle among
The fig leaves of green gushing over no intimate dark.

Enraptured was I by a scarlet A. *hippeastrum*
Blaring its beauty in all four directions to hark
Back to a primitive impulse, a harmony sung
In four measured parts by a sultry awakening lark.

Enthralled was I by a water-filled lady slipper orchid
Enfolding its liquid so lusciously lilac filled up,
And marveled how flowers have powers
massaging the nerves,
Releasing the tensions and stilling the mind's enchirid.
What endearment's embraced in a sun-kissed
with gold buttercup,
Or when dogwood blooms blood-tip their indented
white-petalled curves!

Looking At The Great Painters Through Rose-Colored Glasses

The collection of slides was three decades old.
The colors had turned washed with rose dye
as if viewed through a ruby beholder.

Picasso's blue period was no longer cold.
The Breughel ochres were peach with pink sky,
and flesh became a strawberry shoulder.

So age tints our vision in a way just as bold
to warm our last years till we die
like the sunset's red glow growing older.

Japanese Papers

I have a package of them
somewhere
tucked in a painted wooden chest
hidden and forgotten
for decades.
It's a sampler
of sheets of different weights,
textures, tints,
some streaked
with metallic gold or silver,
waiting
for sumi painting,
inked landscapes,
to piece and paste
onto small scrolls,
or fold
into origami
birds, butterflies,
fans, tiny kites,
boxes,
and little parasols.
I have a box of inks
in miniature bottles,
and Japanese brushes
left in a drawer
for decades
waiting
       waiting
             waiting

The Future

It is summer
and the people
never go out anymore.
It is 120 degrees and the fans
of the air conditioners
whirr like a storm
in the distance
which is caught like the crackle
of an old radio.
They do all their work
and come together
only on their computers.
All the streets and the roads
are emptied like the hills of sand
of the burning Sahara.

Our Romance

Love, put your hands deep
in your pockets
and walk away
whistling.
It's been months of emotions
slow cooking in a Crock-Pot
to crumbles,
my poems becoming tasteless
as flaxseed.
What's left is dribbling like spit
from the corners of the mouths
of the very old.
My heart is a path trodden
hard and smooth by thousands
of hours of silence.
My brain ticks away
a dialogue of endearments
like a secret still corked.
My body manufactures
its sexual excitement
like popcorn left
to get stale in the microwave.
Thanks for the memories.

I Fell In Love With A Fart

At first he seemed
like a dreamy perfume
of orange blossoms, apple blossoms,
hyacinths, and roses.

Then he became a promising scent
of fresh-cut muskmelon,
peaches, and cucumbers,
a summer breeze after rain.

A whiff of vinegar began to creep in,
garlic and onions frying in olive oil,
though inviting, not sweet.

Ah, but then he was dark chocolate,
bananas, and pineapples
creamed in strawberry juice.

Then a dreaded fishy smell
of tuna, clams, and sardines
that came on like salt air
off a tide of dead mackerel
puckered my nose.

But soon he became peanut butter,
black raspberry jam,
and fresh milk.

Alas, then he turned to burned broccoli,
moldy potatoes, aroma
of hot, sweaty armpits,
and old tennis shoes.

My then-pinched, nervous nostrils
were soon soothed and reopened
by freshly cut grass,
mint, bayberry, rosemary, and rhubarb.

They were finally smothered
in a roomful of old men
feasting on chili, pinto beans, and hot peppers,
fire cracking farts like a jackhammer drilling
the stench of old garbage cans
into my heart.

The World Changes Without Your Permission

New construction follows demolition.
A mudroom replaces the sunporch you recall.
The world changes without your permission.

A breakfast you planned with a fellow musician
at a pancake house that was there last fall
(new construction follows demolition)

is missed due to lack of recognition
of a building that is having an overhaul.
The world changes without your permission.

The architecture of a beloved tradition
is cut down with the uncaring wrecking ball.
New construction follows demolition.

Your heart is torn at the sad omission
of trees or the ceramic cows along a wall.
The world changes without your permission.

And what is left is a stoic submission
that only your memories endure at all
when new construction follows demolition
and the world changes without your permission.

"Moon Cabbage"

That's what Cora called the kale,
that green and purple ball of frills
and ruffles, more a decoration than a meal.

"It looks like it comes from the moon,"
and here "the moon" is not that ball of rocks
and empty real estate our astronauts set foot on.

"The moon" is that romantic orb of memory and light
whose shadows suggest a face shining and smiling
down from the dark and distant galaxy of night

on loving couples dancing, singing, kissing,
with voices low from lips on faces,
silhouetted figures softly lit and shadowed
by the satin sheen of moon glow.

Two Moon Haiku

An appliquéd moon
on your blue jeans hip pocket
keeps winking at me.

Magnificent moon,
white flounder that floats slowly through
dark deeps of heaven.

Haiku In Black And White

Soft fur on rough bark
an albino squirrel hugs
dark trunk of white oak

Subzero Haiku

Down under a bridge
a man wrapped in plastic bags
dies. Who cares? Who cries?

To Lester Teeple Who Sold His Farm To Panasonic

Your big sixteen-sided barn
waits near steel and concrete,
wearing away in the wind.

Haiku On The Completed Life Of Poet Clyde Weaver

In a parked car prayed,
a weaver of peace and love;
unseen scythe reaped faith.

The Intense Light Of Jesus Christ, A Parable About Darkness

While seated in the dentist's chair
under the intense light,
my black slacks turn white.

Lines After Reading Elaine Equi

Her form reminded me of music boxes:
the lines that rhythmically repeat
as the figures curtsy, bow,
each follows in its time the windup pattern.

The lines that rhythmically repeat
to take turns with the new conceit,
each follows in its time the windup pattern.
The milkmaid moves her hands under the cow.

To take turns with the new conceit,
the country dancers twirl and stop;
the milkmaid moves her hand under the cow.
The cow lifts up her head.

The country dancers twirl and stop
just as the fiddler saws his bow.
The cow lifts up her head,
and then the owl flies from the barn.

Just as the fiddler saws his bow
the cat jumps out the window,
and then the owl flies from the barn,
"Who-who, who-who"; the rabbit runs.

The cat jumps out the window
More slowly as the tune winds down.
"Whoo-whoo, whoo-whooo"; the rabbit runs
or rather crawls as with a limp.

More slowly as the tune winds down,
the tinkling falters, fades,
or rather crawls as with a limp
as I sense my advancing age.

And the tinkling falters, fades
like the figure stiffens, bows,
as I sense my advancing age.
Her form reminded me of music boxes.

God Is In The Details

"I give you the end of a golden string, only wind it into a ball, it will lead you in at Heaven's gate built in Jerusalem's wall."

—William Blake

Okay, let's start with a golden string, the kind
you buy at Hallmark Cards to tie your gifts
at Christmas. And this Christmas I did find
just such a golden string around a gift
for me. Metallic chevroned scales twined
as thin as baby snakeskin's sparkling thrift,
and taken in, I struggled to unwind
tight knots and rolled it round my hand,
then shifted on to other things. Just where
I put it last, I can't recall, and it's not
in the obvious places. But, friend,
do I need the actual string, or just
the recollection? Then, if thought replaces,
extends the ends, where does it lead?
Untied, a knot of life once freed, resides inside.

Final Good-Bye

I want to die as gently as a leaf falls,
and crawl into the shroud like a child
falls asleep in loving arms exhausted;
I want to die like petals fall from roses,
and sunsets blend their tints into the sea;
I want to die as quiet as the silence
after notes slow at the end of a melody.

Jane Sassaman's Exuberant Dandelions

You celebrated dandelions in your quilt "Weeds."
I like to blow them when they turn to seeds.
As appropriately for this old grey hair
As that might be, I've not the energy
Nor time to stitch globed webs of balls of air
In all their intricate design. Not me.
Not now though I am so excited by
Your life, your art, your use of flowers. My
Imagination travels back to Virginia,
Where I sit in a park in Richmond painting
In oil on wood the dogwood flower's fleeting
Last hurrah before the anthracnose plague
Sweeps sadly through the Southern woodland's shade,
And from that decades-old wood panel draw
My templates for a quilt with praise and awe.

Good-Bye To Mrs. Goodjohn

She had a museum in her classroom.
     She taught her class to mind.
She put each child beneath her wing.
     Behind her stern was kind.

She shouldered burdens only teachers know
     And Kelvyn is the less.
I weep inside to see her go
     Whose duty was to bless

With knowledge and with character
     And caring for each other,
Each student safe under her eye
     Like sister and like brother.

Not knowing history is to repeat
     The errors of the past,
But the lessons that her students learned,
     That legacy will last.

Waving Farewell To Eleanor Wicks

Math is a ladder for us to climb
From the real to the abstract,
A system of logic so sublime
Built upon number and fact.
You were schooled in its harmony,
A master of connection and tact.

You knew how to solve hard equations
And every elegant proof.
You knew the algorithms of persuasions,
Yet you were never aloof.

You guided us so profoundly
Like Descartes' magic grid,
That we functioned in love all around you,
Blessed in all that we did.

No one could count as well as you
The rigors of our teamwork
On this frontline of civilization,
And the duties that we can't shirk.

You taught your students to build bridges,
That when broken could be built again.
Your aim was so pure and unswerving
That your strength was to the power of ten.

You picked us up, kept us going,
When we feared to falter or fall,
And the memory of that will keep glowing,
A gift to the hearts of us all.

We are sad that we won't see you daily
Serving our needs and that sticks
Like Pythagoras and pi still prevailing,
Like none other, beloved Eleanor Wicks.

Solitary Passage

to the tune of Lloyd-Webber's "Memory"

Rain falls
on the streets of Chicago,
and the sidewalks are sheeted
with wet litter, debris.
The streetlamps
reflect their watery shine
in an echo
of design.

The old high school
looms ahead in the darkness,
still awaiting the new dawn
not yet begun.
I will enter
becoming time's washrag again
squeezed and twisted
by the sand.

Still songs
swell my heart as I'm walking,
float my spirit above all
the dark damp and decay.
Disappointment
drips to fill up my day,
but this morning
is melody.

Song For Allegra Podrovsky
Who Gave Her All

How do I play this song for Allegra?
With a glee club singing double forte?
With all the stops pulled out on the organ?
With the band and orchestra surging like an ocean
Of sounding crescendos and a crash of cymbals?

Or like a soaring aria floating pure,
Sung by a lyric soprano with lilting tremolos?
Or plucked like the sweet and soothing strings of the harp?
Or the happy piping of the piccolo for a wee lady
Who possessed the gift of music and the making of it?

Like the tinkling sound of the bell choir?
Or the smooth flowing melody of the flute?
Or on the wings of the violins and cellos?
How to sing the praises of Allegra
Who gave her all to Kelvyn Park High School?

Who shared so generously and sacrificially
With her students all these years her gift of music
To lift their hearts and souls the rest of their lives
Warmed by the memories of the musical awards,
The drum and bugle corps contests they won.

She taught them to play their instruments together
To achieve harmony and beauty as a whole.
And not just the students, but the teachers too.
She brought us the gains of the union's battles
Info we were ignorant of when abused by an uncaring system.

She gave her all, her time, her talent, her skills,
Her knowledge, her health, her passion.
She told me when once she was in New Orleans,
She heard a steel drum band play the famous overture
To Rossini's great opera *William Tell.*

So I would want a host of heavenly angels
And all the orchestras of heaven play now
The final orgasmic jubilant ending
Of that great opera, the joyful cry:
"Liberty comes down from heaven!"
For her last *Pomp and Circumstance.*

A Hymn To Subtraction

The zero point is an opened door
on an up-and-down or back-and-forth line
where more can be less, and less can be more.

You may think addition is life's full design:
another room, child, car, money, more of what's mine.
But life proves that zero is an open door

where as numbers get higher with the negative sign
then it's debit and debt and aging's decline
for more can be less, when less was once more.

What is wealth but to distance oneself from the poor
for the sum in addition depends on the sign
and riches add bolts away from the door.

Subtract some burdens, relationships, chores,
painful sad memories, and the line comes divine
when more can be less, and less can be more.

Oh, to be a child and see only the shine
in the sorrow, the loss, the plummet, the soar
when the zero point is an open door
and more can mean less, and less can mean more.

I Cannot Live With You, But I Can Live

I cannot live with you, but I can live
As long as daffodils herald each spring,
Nor give myself to you, but I can give,

As long as I am needed somewhere and received
In all my weakness, woe, and silly laughing.
I cannot live with you, but I can live.

Though I shall want you always and will bleed
To see you, I cannot put you in a painting,
Nor give myself to you, but I can give

Myself to others, as I am able for their need
Is vast as famine, as everyday as greed and beating.
I cannot live with you, but I can live.

Though crazed, cracked, and broken, I am freed
By God from vain desire's distress, the grieving
To give myself to you. Still, I can give,

Go on and do by hints and signs He seeds
His dark creation, all I can, though blooming,
Would give myself to you. Still I can give.
I cannot live with you, but I can live.

The Girl With The Golden Hair

I remember the sunshine everywhere
Though the wind was chill and the day was grey
When I walked with the girl with the golden hair.

The trees in the park were stark and bare
To silence the chatter that I would say
Though I remember the sunshine everywhere.

It seemed the wild geese turned to stare
Unwilling to scatter when we stepped their way
When I walked with the girl with the golden hair.

I felt a presence through all the air
Of wings and arms and a rose bouquet;
I remember sunshine everywhere.

Did a heavenly host descend a stair
To tune up the trees and the breezes play
As I walked with the girl with the golden hair?

When my days are drab and I sink in a chair
And long for some verse to ride me away,
I remember the sunshine everywhere
When I walked with the girl with the golden hair.

Her Hair Is Full Of Night

Her hair is full of night
with strands of silver stars
that light the way to morning
and the day.

Her face is full of dusk
whose veils shade the trees
where blossoms flare like candles
in the air.

Her hand is full of evening
to cool the fevered forehead
and heal with a heaven
you can feel.

Her voice is full of water
for the cracked and thirsty land
of overheating hearts
in city streets.

Her hair is full of night
with strings of tiny pearls
that grew from pains into
her art of truth.

Cinquain

Shells
Sea sprayed, whorled,
sink in swirls
serene as sand jewels
shells

Rondeau On The Suicide Of Abby Hoffman, Sixties Activist

Steal this poem and say it's yours
that night you wrote it dead on drugs
scrawled on the nation's stripes and stars
while spinning albums by the Fugs.
The neon flashes: NO MORE WARS!

"Light my fire!" scream the Doors,
but all your women washed ashore;
each left in turn for all the tugs
upon their hearts—the last encores.
Steal this poem.

The pig for president still mugs;
the mock on the convention roars;
the whole world watches you and hugs
the TV screen; the courtroom soars
to heaven where Judge Hoffman lugs
his bad boy home in Woodstock lore.
Steal this poem.

Reflections On Longfellow's "The Village Blacksmith" This Earth Day, 1992

Under the spreading chestnut tree
killed by the chestnut blight.
The baby trees sprout from the roots,
a sad and painful sight,
for they will die from that same blight
before they're sapling grown;
their human counterpart is found
in every city and town.

The village smithy stands.
My great-grandfather worked the forge,
a flinty, wiry man,
bending the iron into lucky horseshoes
for the horses of Clarington.

The smith a mighty man is he
as mighty as was that chestnut tree,
and while botanists hybridize to find
a blight-free chestnut, never mind
looking to find a blacksmith.

Divine Intervention

"As you have described the situation,
I would give your mother a year
before she has a nervous breakdown,
and then your brother would go back
to his old gang and stealing cars,
and when they are arrested,
let's hope the judge sees
his real problem and has him put
in psychiatric care.
But you seem to be okay."

"What is there that I can do to change that?"

"I don't see that there is anything
that you can do, but if your mother
would come in and talk with me . . ."

"I've already asked,
and she waved it away."

"Well, then, I don't see that
there is anything you can do."

The door that had the words
SUMMIT COUNTY COUNSELLOR
lettered on the opaque glass window
slammed as I left.

Some where in my wanderings
with troubled spirit and despairing thoughts
(Nothing I can do, nothing I can do)
up and down the streets between
the Summit County offices
and the campus
of the University of Akron,
I realized that I had laid down
my big straw bag with all my papers
I had graded and my record book

for my student teaching classes
in English at Central High Summer School.
But where was it?
I retraced my steps again and again,
but could not find it.
"Well, that's it.
That is certainly it.
I'm not okay, mister.
Now how am I to face those kids
tomorrow without their papers,
and my critic teacher without
the records of attendance and grades?
No, I am not okay.
I can do nothing to solve the nightmare
of my mother and my brother,
and now I am too incompetent
to even teach.

I will fail, I will fail,
and sink into the hell
of humiliation,
waitressing stuck with my mother
and my brother watching it all
go to the awful end,
and I've no money to support myself,
except go back to Grandma,
and endure her wrath and disappointment,
and making me account for every minute,
and keeping me at home when I should be
in the library.
What next? To lose my waitress job?
Already it is hard for me to focus,
when I want so much to be in a classroom.
No, I'm not okay.
And why not just end it all?
I can't face tomorrow,
I just can't.
I can't make it all come right.
I just can't find them.
If I'm careful and see that the street's deserted,
I can crawl around the fence

and hold on to the railing until I'm just above
the racing cars below the bridge
over the expressway.
I'm here and it's so scary to look down
at the cars that have messed up my brother.
I'll close my eyes and count to ten,
and then let go."

Before I got to ten,
strong arms grabbed me
and pulled me back over the railing,
and I stood there staring at three persons,
staring back and asking,
"Are you okay?
Should we call an ambulance?"
"No, no, I am okay now.
Thank you for saving me.
Thank you, thank you,
I'm okay now."
And they were gone.
There was no car,
and I looked up and down the street.
They were gone.
Were they from earth or heaven?
For the street was not the same
as I walked into the wind,
and heard the carillon,
First Presbyterian.
"God does not want me to die.
God does not want me to die!
I'll go see Dr. Watt and tell him
that I lost all my teaching stuff,
and what then should I do?"
And all the sacred music played,
the hymns of the carillon.
"God does not want me to die."

To A Teen Who Thinks Suicide Is The Solution

Before you swallow that bottle of pills,
Before you shoot that gun,
Or step off the curb to meet that Corvette,
Stop and call someone!

Before you drop from that bridge railing,
Before you stab that knife
Or close up the car with the motor running,
Stop and decide to choose life.

Choose life though the pain is so stabbing
You can hardly breathe or cry;
Choose life though in facing tomorrow
A part of you must die.

And I give you a rainbow promise
For I have been where you are
That there will come a tomorrow
That will shine in your heart like a star.

So don't listen to cruel despair's voices
That tell you this must be the end,
You're too young to know all the choices,
Or the good things that bad things can send.

You're too young to know how life cycles
And spirals from pain into joy,
And that life is a stranger adventure
Than you ever dreamed as a boy.

If you think defeat's all life will give you,
So why bother to try anymore,
Remember what we know about winter,
And the end of that cold corridor.

Remember that you only see partly,
And you may not be seeing it right,
That your story will surely end better,
So have faith and keep up the fight.

The Love Of Jesus Christ

The love of Jesus Christ is always there
when human love transforms into a snare
and an enchanting dream becomes a lie
and there's no answer to the question why
I've been deceived again and I can't bear

repeatedly to suffer wounds to tear
and bleeding stain the tears from pain I'd swear
there's some demonic sadist who'd deny
the love of Jesus Christ,

and this satanic spirit's fixed his stare
on me. But then a voice comes from somewhere,
the phone, a friend, a thought, a hymn, a sigh,
a song, a poem, a verse of scripture makes reply,
and I am touched, made new with healing care,
the love of Jesus Christ.

SONGS

Forgiveness Is The Fragrance

"Forgiveness is the fragrance of the violet
upon the heel that crushes it."

When the violet is stomped,
and the leaves and stems smashed,
still the roots are secure underground.

When the heart's hopes are tramped,
and its fondest dreams trashed,
still new life in Christ can abound.

The Bunny And The Wolf-Child

A bunny and a wolf-child
    Rowed across a lake
In a leaky rowboat,
    And nothing did they take
To bail out the water rising
    In the bottom of the boat,
Like a couple life preservers
    To help keep them afloat.

The bunny sat high in the stern
    While the wolf-child worked the oars
With the rowboat sinking lower
    As the water level soars.
The bunny took to moaning low
    That the trip was a mistake
Especially to omit a pail
    Before they crossed the lake.

The wolf-child gave a wild look
    For he knew how to swim.
If Bunny drowned, she would be
    A tasty meal for him.
Bunny clung fast to her seat,
    And seeing the farther shore,
Wondered if they'd make it there
    As the boat sank lower and lower.

Wolf-child rowed slower now,
 Claiming that he was tired.
Bunny urged him to exert
 And wondered what she'd hired.
Panicked she gnawed the wood seat free
 In time to float away,
As the boat went underwater
 But wolf-child chose to stay.

He hung onto each floating oar
 Since the boat had dropped below.
Then he began to swim to catch
 The wood seat floating slow,

Bunny sat there frightened,
 As she saw him fast advance,
Then spying a swimming otter,
 Decided to take a chance.

She sprang onto the otter's back
 And the otter did not dive,
But sped toward the nearest shoreline
 With the bunny still alive.
The wolf-child watched his meal hop
 Onto the bank and flee,
And the bunny's lucky rescue
 Should comfort you and me.

A Time To Live And A Time To Die

In the evening of the day
    while several rabbits jumped at play
one rabbit turned to look my way
    so that I stopped my walk to stay
and watch it slowly hop and stray
    from its companions hopping away
with their dancing energy display
    into the twilight of early May.

But as it hopped it coughed to say
    I'm sick and need your caring way
of attending to my call and pray
    that you will take me home today.
But I though moved did turn away.
    My pet rabbits in cages lay,
and its snuffles would each one slay
    in an epidemic disarray.

I saw its hope die at my nay.
    I saw it weary turn away,
and slowly the lively troupe obey
    coughing in its weakened grey
acceptance as the night owl's prey.
    Reluctant I went on my way
with tears at the unending clay
    that frustrates what we'd make okay,

Spring Bird Blues

Song Sparrows,
Spare me your songs;
This wrong is past mending.

Mourning Doves,
Moan in the morning;
I mourn with each new daffodil.

Red-breasted Robins.
Go cheer up the rain;
This breast burns red with pain.

Chattering Blue Jays,
Flash feathers and fly;
Bluer than you flow my days.

It's Too Late

"We're going to drive you crazy!"
my students taunt me, rude and lazy.
Laughing, I answer and avoid the bait,
"You can't, I am already. It's too late."

"He is going to break your heart!"
the inner voices warn. "He will depart."
Sighing, I shield me from that stabbing fate,
"My heart's already broken. It's too late."

"I'll make you die in deep despair,"
says a dark voice with a hateful stare.
Smiling, I pray to God and wait
for my Savior's love is not too late.

When I First Fell In Love With You

When I first fell in love with you
the air was full of kisses soft,
songs gentle as rose petals flew,
awesome raptures ballooned aloft.

The air was full of kisses soft,
defeated longings, dead dreams awoke,
awesome raptures ballooned aloft,
endearing words were often spoke.

Defeated longings, dead dreams awoke,
Springtime joy in autumn bloomed,
endearing words were often spoke,
hopes swelled like new life in the womb.

Springtime joy in autumn bloomed,
rainbows rose up in my heart,
hopes swelled like new life in the womb,
whispers promised poems and art.

Rainbows rose up in my heart,
years, wrinkles, gray hair lost in mirth,
whispers promised poems and art,
seas of happiness washed the earth.

Years, wrinkles, gray hair lost in mirth,
cathedrals of fulfillment called,
seas of happiness washed the earth,
embraces of angel arms enthralled.

Cathedrals of fulfillment called,
songs gentle as rose petals flew,
embraces of angel arms enthralled,
when I first fell in love with you.

Your Hands

I love to see you move your hands
like couples dancing to your words
that every heartbeat understands.
I love to see you move your hands
like caravans caress the sands,
like brushstrokes or a flight of birds.
I love to see you move your hands
like couples dancing to your words.

Dancing Song

I'm dancing away to the sunset
   clothed in red velvet and pearls.
I'm dancing away in the twilight.
    Come, take my hand as we twirl.

I'm dancing away in the starshine
   clothed in transparent blue veils.
I'm dancing away in the moonlight
    that shines on my silvery curls.

I'm dancing away in the darkness
   clothed in black velvet and night.
I'm dancing away to the distance.
    I'm dancing away out of sight.

The Black Swan

You have to be
　　in the land down under
If you want to see
　　the startling wonder
When a black swan flies
　　into the sunrise,
Its darkness defined
　　by the glowing skies.

A white swan lives
　　in the blue of day,
But a black swan gives
　　a dashing display
Of the power of black
　　as the sunset bars
To a golden track
　　for an ebony star.

The Song Sparrow

O little bird of liquid song,
of warbling melodies and trills
amazing me with awesome thrills
so purely musically strong.

You sang for me within the tree
that branches near my window.
My morning eyes searched for the bough
that held your being brown and wee.

Alas, you flew away but left
the echo in my ear and soul
which lifted me to beauty whole
resplendent with this one-time gift.

The Song Of The Cicadas

After seventeen years
Deep underground
They come out to mate
With a mighty sound.

It's a high-pitched roar
That surges and slows
That rises and rolls
That ebbs and flows.

It commands your attention
Though you're deep in thought
like the whine of a siren
Or the scream of a shot.

It's like all the violins
On all the earth
Sustained but one note
For all they're worth.

Like a majestic soprano
Piercing all ears
With a high note on hold
That shatters chandeliers.

What are they singing?
"Come to me dear.
I'm here but one moment,
Then I'll disappear.

It's only an instant
Of fleeting time,
A rhythm, a passion,
A climax, a rhyme."

Song Of The Summer Rain

As I lie down at night,
I hear a storm start up,
the pings, the flash of light,
the drops erupt.

I feel the air go cool
and hear the whoosh of trees
that bend and sway, a tool
of wind and breeze.

The music mends my soul;
my senses welcome rain.
It will fill up the hole
and wash the stain

of days that dry my mind
with sand the minutes spin
and lacking moisture, grind
to let dust in.

But with the cleansing rain
that gives all plants a drink,
strange fancies flush my brain;
ideas link.

The raindrops soothe my dreams
like nectar feeds the bird;
what was forgotten seems
like voices heard.

They whisper words of songs
that only raindrops sing,
a promise that belongs
within a ring.

From The Lunar Astronauts

The astronauts have been to the moon,
and they've shown that it's rocky and cold;
it's barren and dry and no robins fly,
no caterpillar spins a cocoon.

The astronauts have been to the moon,
and it's not a romantic place,
no nightingale's tune, no roses in June,
though it shines with a manlike face.

The astronauts have been to the moon,
but they only stayed for a visit,
no welcoming hands, no beating brass bands,
but they answered the question "What is it?"

The astronauts have been to the moon,
but no one went back with his wife.
It's left in the sky for there they would die;
down here on earth is life.

Dream Of A Summer Night

Lay your head upon my lap
  And let your spirit soar.
The stars above are music notes
  Dancing in a score.

Listen to the cicadas hum
  And the crickets out of sight,
The owl hoots in the woods nearby,
  The sounds of a summer night.

The lightning bugs flit and fly,
  Dots flickering in the dark,
And I would sing of Jesus' love,
  And sweet romance's spark.

Spring Song To
A Man Who Is Eighty

Can your heart still burst like buds
When eighty spring times have come round,
Or are the tears close to a flood
Of April raindrops on the ground?

Can your eyes still see the blooms
Despite your long life's wear and tear,
Or does the sight remind you of
The friends that are no longer there?

Can you rejoice with wonder still
At the rebirth the springtime brings,
Or does your history's sad times fill
Your voice and weary what you sing?

I pray that you not fear that this
Fleeting March may be your last,
And that this present springtime's bliss
Outshines the eighty that have passed.

Spirit Music

When my small spirit swells and soars
Like the church organ without stops,
Or an orchestra of strings and horns,

I know that heaven's sliding door
Has opened on the mountaintops
Haloed in suns of early morns.

And I rise up in a downpour
Of angels and birds from the treetops,
And praise the Lord with faith reborn.

Stomping Out The Grapes

A satyr and a nymph
are stomping out the grapes.
The hairy hooves, bare feet
are stained in purple sweet.

A young swain and a maid
are stomping out the grapes.
His breeches and her skirts
are soaked with wine-red spurts.

A farmer and his bride
are stomping out the grapes.
His pant legs and her knees
are bathed in burgundy.

An old man and his wife
are stomping out the grapes.
His worn shirt and her blouse
are sprayed with seedless souse.

Come and join me, love
in stomping out the grapes.
We'll mash the balls of puce
And drink the luscious juice.

My Song Was Gone

Yesterday
my song was gone.
All I could do was pray.

Yesterday
my mood unglued,
and all around was gray.

Yesterday
my eyes were sighs
that would not go away.

But all of that was yesterday.

Now today
I heard the birds,
and saw a rose bouquet.

Now today
my heart's Mozart
as light as orange soufflé.

Now today
I feel ideal,
and life's a free buffet.

For I dreamed you loved me today.

The Juicy Joy Of Spring's First Rain

You feel it come
      As the weather warms;
You feel the sun
      Reach out its arms,
And the water-laden clouds
      Let go:

O, dance with me in the juicy rain!
Don't hide behind that windowpane.
Come out and shout and wash your brain!
Prance with joy like a whooping crane!
Come dance with me in the juicy rain.

You see it peep
      In the melting snow;
You see it creep
      From the ground below,
And the water-laden clouds
      Let go:

O, dance with me in the juicy rain!
Don't hide behind that windowpane.
Come out and shout and wash your brain!
Prance with joy like a whooping crane!
Come dance with me in the juicy rain!

Rain Song

I love the muttering thunder
when lightning splits asunder
the black skies.

I love the splattering patter
of raindrops as they batter
and baptize.

I love the smell of moisture
in the soaked air cleaned and pure
as it dries.

I love when plants and flowers
drink up the drip of showers
as they rise.

I love you folding the umbrella,
a damp but smiling fella
with wet eyes.

If I Could Jump Rope With The Wind

If I could jump rope with the wind
And tap dance on a cloud,
If I could hop-scotch with the sun
And spin the world around,
If I could climb up a rainbow
And swing away to the moon,
If I could scatter like lightning
And crack like the thunder at noon,
Then I could sleep deep in the rain
And caress the shadows of sight,
And never know canyons of pain
Or the whip of a blinding kite.

"There Is No Love Unreturned"

How wise are these words of Walt Whitman;
How true do they ring in the spring.
Each bloom sings the blest affirmation;
Each leaf shouts the glad celebration:
"There is no love unreturned."

No matter what cruel disappointment
Has seized your sad soul in this life,
No matter what passions you've squandered
On what seemed to give back only strife,
"There is no love unreturned."

The pay is rolled inside the giving;
The prize is slipped into the loving;
It's found in the faith when you've yearned;
It's the hope that's within all that's spurned:
"There is no love unreturned."

Glosa For My Son

I wandered early
Through a maze of halls
and vaulted ceilings rising up
to hold a hovering Spirit

from "Seminary, a poem" by Seamus Enright

I wandered early
In my mind
Awakened at five-thirty
From a dream that seemed unkind
And was ending poorly.
My thoughts traveled far to find
What was meant obscurely
Though in bed was I reclined
As I wandered early

Through a maze of halls
I struggled for connections
Between the vision that recalls
The losing of directions
And the fear of what befalls
Without divine reflections
Unwinding from the balls
Of thread tied to protections
Through a maze of halls

and vaulted ceilings rising up
From memories of cathedrals
Where I had stood looking up
To see the arches curve the walls
Like giant hands in prayer cup
Like trunks of trees grown so tall

As the sound of singing echoes up
As the surging organ soaring falls
From the vaulted ceilings rising up

to hold a hovering Spirit
A transparent angel's outspread wings
Clothed like a cloud with sunrise near it
An umbrella or a shield that springs
From unseen powers that stretch and steer it
Over the shifting emotion's swings
So there will be no cause to fear it
And free the heart that gives and sings
to hold a hovering Spirit

The Sea Of Love

There is a long unconscious sea
that ebbs and flows continuously
in all of us and especially
through you and me.

While some pollute the water's mirror,
a heavenly presence makes it clear
and clean so we can persevere,
and no poison fear.

I send this loving message through
to help make every dream come true
and wash each pain with honeydew.
May God bless you.